Odin
Happy Trails
So nice to meet ya
— Chica

THRU-HIKING THE APPALACHIAN TRAIL

100 TIPS, TRICKS, TRAPS, AND FACTS

Jen Beck Seymour "Chica"
Greg Seymour "Sunsets"

Odin,
Great meeting you. Keep on Hiking
— Sunsets

Ohio Trails!
Hope to meet you
So nice to meet you.
Circus Jacket Co

Cali,
God bless you, keep in
His

Copyright © 2018 Greg Seymour Jen Beck Seymour

All rights reserved.

All product and company names are trademarks™ or registered® trademarks of their respective holders. The trademark holders are not affiliated with the authors of this book and do not endorse this book.

ALSO BY JEN BECK SEYMOUR

Costa Rica Chica

Life Outside the Cubicle

Costa Rica Chica Cookbook

Grecia, Costa Rica

ALSO BY GREG SEYMOUR

Living in and Visiting Costa Rica

Costa Rica Curious

TABLE OF CONTENTS

INTRODUCTION
HIKER JARGON
I. KNOW BEFORE YOU GO
II. GEARING UP
III. MONEY, MONEY, MONEY
IV. SHELTER ME
V. BODY OF WORK
VI. CREATURE FEATURE
VII. PEEING, POOPING, PERIODS & PRIVIES
VIII. SPECIFIC SPECIFICATIONS
IX. FUEL & MAINTENANCE
X. LOOSE ENDS
XI. WHAT'S STOPPING YOU?
CLOSING
BONUS – GEAR LISTS

INTRODUCTION

"So, have you read *A Walk in the Woods?*"

This question inevitably was asked of us when we informed friends and family we were going to hike the Appalachian Trail (AT). This, of course, is interchangeable with the book *Wild (*even though *Wild* takes place on the opposite coast of Bryson's account). And, why not? These two tales of long distance "walking on a whim" captured the world's attention and have convinced many that the pursuit is feasible for everyone.

Indeed, the two books are among the reasons completing a "thru-hike" (hiking a whole trail within 12 months) occupies a high position on the bucket lists of many angling to amble in the wilderness for several months. This, despite the fact neither author completed their thru-hike of the Appalachian Trail or the Pacific Crest Trail, respectively. However, *we did*.

Our journey on the Appalachian Trail – through 14 states and over 2,189.8 miles – started at Amicalola Falls, Georgia on March 22, 2017 and ended on Mount Katahdin, Maine on September 16, 2017.

We were a peculiar demographic to complete the epic journey. First, we hiked in our mid-40s while the majority of long-distance wanderers were much younger with most in their 20s. Secondly, we were a couple, and there were very few of these animals on the trail. It's hard enough for a single person to dodge ailments, injury, and the emotional toll of the trail, let alone two to finish together. Thirdly, prior to our hike, we had not spent more than three consecutive nights in a tent – ever. So, on paper we were unlikely to complete the trail in one go. But we beat the odds and finished together.

The percentage of finishers is in flux from year to year. Typically, only 25-30% of those who start hiking the trail with the intention of completing the entire trek in a 12-month period complete it. We went from backpacking neophytes to experts in the span of 179 days.

The purpose of this book is to pass along some of the knowledge we gained during our thru-hike to help you successfully plan and implement *your* hike.

Thru-Hiking the Appalachian Trail – 100 Tips, Tricks, Traps, and Facts is not meant to be a comprehensive guide. Rather, we will provide an overview of the trail, as well as some of the minutia that leads to a successful completion.

Writing a book together is not the same as hiking together. To keep the peace, we split up the chapters between us, so we each have our own unique voice.

We designate who wrote which chapter in the chapter title. Also, keep in mind when reading our stories or while considering the geography that we thru-hiked the trail NOBO (northbound) from Georgia to Maine.

Following this introduction is a list of typical slang terms used by the thru-hiking community. Beginning in chapter one, the first use of each term will be shown in quotes with a brief parenthetical definition.

Not only will you learn about the AT and what life is like on the trail, but you will also learn tips for budgeting, planning meals, dealing with bears and other pests, following park regulations, selecting gear, and oh, so much more!

We documented our trip, almost daily, on the following social media platforms:

YouTube.com/AppalachianTrailTales
AppalachianTrailTales.com
Facebook.com/AppalachianTrailTales
Instagram.com/AppalachianTrailTales

Please follow us on the above social media pages as we continue to explore the AT and other long trails in the U.S. and abroad (up next, the Camino de Santiago in Spain).

Hiking the Appalachian Trail can be life-changing. It certainly changed ours. Knowledge, a sense of adventure, a healthy dose of humor, and endless tenacity are all needed to complete this epic journey. Good luck with your research. We wish you the best for your journey on the Appalachian Trail, and as the saying goes:

> **"The journey of a thousand miles begins with a single step."**
> *~ Lao Tzu*

Rock On and Walk On,

~ Sunsets & Chica

HIKER JARGON

Hikers on the Appalachian Trail are a distinct community with their own culture. For instance, hikers go by nicknames instead of their real names, hitchhiking happens all the time, and sharing hotel rooms with virtual strangers is the norm, as is going without a shower for days. Alongside this different lifestyle is a unique jargon used among hikers, which you won't find in any dictionary. Here's our version of the most-heard words on the trail and their meanings.

2,000-Miler: A term used by the ATC to signify a thru-hiker – even though the complete distance, which changes every year, is longer than 2,000 miles.

ATC: The Appalachian Trail Conservancy, a nonprofit organization dedicated to the conservation of the Appalachian Trail.

AT Guide (**"Awol's *Guide*"**): The most-used guidebook on the Appalachian Trail, comes in e-book (pdf) and paper-book format (northbound or southbound, bound book or loose-leaf), by David "Awol" Miller.

Bear bag: Bag used for food and anything that

smells, which is hung every night out of reach of bears and other animals.

Blazes: There are several different blazes along the Appalachian Trail, both physical (blazes) and metaphorical (blazing):

--*White blaze:* A 2" x 6" vertical rectangle painted on trees, rocks or signposts showing the way on the Appalachian Trail.

--*Double white blaze:* Two white blazes, one above the other, signify an intersection or turn coming up. Two offset white blazes indicate a turn coming up, turning in the direction of the top blaze.

--*Blue blaze:* A 2" x 6" vertical rectangle on trees, signifying trails leading off the Appalachian Trail going to shelters, water sources, views or bad-weather routes.

--*Yellow blazing:* Bypassing parts of the Appalachian Trail by road (the "yellow" comes from the middle yellow line of the road).

--*Aqua blazing:* Bypassing parts of the Appalachian Trail by canoe, boat or kayak, typically through the Shenandoah National Park section of the AT.

--*Deli blazing:* One who tries to hit all of the delis (especially in NJ and NY) along the Appalachian

Trail.

--Green blazing: One who smokes (marijuana) their way up the trail having frequent "safety meetings" with fellow green blazers.

--Pink blazing: A male thru-hiker trying to catch up with a female thru-hiker by clues left in the shelter trail logs/journals.

--Banana blazing: A female thru-hiker trying to catch up with a male thru-hiker by clues left in the shelter trail logs/journals.

--Silk blazing: Being the first hiker on the trail in the early morning usually means you are clearing all the "silk" (spider webs) from the trail.

Blow-down: Tree or limb that has fallen across the trail.

Bounce box: A box you use and keep sending ahead from post office to post office (*i.e.,* might contain a large bottle of painkillers, *etc.*, that you only want to carry a small of amount of on the trail. You take a handful for your next days out in the woods and send the large, heavy bottle forward).

Bubble: A large number of hikers hiking together for a period of time, usually starting and ending at the same campsites each night or slightly staggered.

Buff: A soft material, similar to a bandana, but sewn together so it is tubular. Can be worn in a multitude of ways on the head, around the neck, or around the wrist. Protects from sun, absorbs sweat, and covers ears in cold weather.

Cowboy camping: Camping without a shelter over you, so you are exposed to the night sky.

Day hiker: Person who is hiking for just the day.

Embrace the suck: You will hear this almost daily. It means that some days absolutely suck – with rain, heat, body aches, *etc.* – so you need to embrace these things to get through the day.

Flip-flop: A hike that begins in one direction, then at some point changes direction (*i.e.*, hiker starts in the middle at Harpers Ferry, WV and goes north to Katahdin, ME, then flips back to Harpers Ferry and goes south to Springer Mountain, GA). Even if someone starts out NOBO or SOBO, they can always flip. An example of a common strategy is for the NOBO hiker to flip up to Katahdin in the summer. This provides for cooler weather when naturally they would be going through New Jersey and New York, two states that can be extremely hot and humid.

Gap: A low spot along the trail, usually going

through a parking lot or crossing a road.

Guthooks: The most-used app for cellphones for the entire Appalachian Trail. Runs on GPS and does not need cell data (we used it while our phones were in airplane mode).

Harpers Ferry: The psychological and traditional halfway point in West Virginia, where the Appalachian Trail Conservancy is located (not the actual half-way point, as this changes every year, but close to it).

Hiker box: A box or container at hostels, hotels, and places in town where hikers can donate unwanted items (food, clothing, gear) and other hikers can take from it freely.

Hiker midnight: Typically around 9 p.m., an etiquette observed by being quiet and dimming the lights.

Hiker trash: An affectionate term used to describe long-distance hikers who become so accustomed to the simple life on the trail that they exhibit the sometimes socially unacceptable habits associated with it (*i.e.*, doing laundry by hand in the hotel bathtub, not showering for days and smelling like it, growing a full and untrimmed beard, finding unwrapped candy on the trail and eating it because they are too hungry to care about where it came from).

Hiker hunger: Refers to the more-than-usual hunger of hikers, generally lasting for most of a thru-hike, since hikers burn so many calories each day.

Hostel: An establishment along the trail that has bunks, showers, laundry, resupply and mail-drop options for hikers. A hostel will sometimes have private rooms available as well.

Hut: In the White Mountains of New Hampshire, there are huts where any hiker can make reservations to stay (usually pricey for thru-hikers). Price includes dinner and breakfast. Thru-hikers can often "work for stay" at the huts (though that means sleeping on the floor of the dining hall with people walking by all night to visit the restroom).

HYOH: "Hike Your Own Hike," a term said to fellow thru-hikers often, meaning hike the AT the way you want to, and don't necessarily do what everyone else does.

Key Swap: A way of thru-hiking the Appalachian Trail that involves two people and a car. Example: Each day, Hiker 1 starts out on the day's trail section from the south. Hiker 2 then drives to the north end of the section, parks the car at the trailhead, and starts walking south. When they meet in the middle, Hiker 2 hands the car keys to Hiker 1. When the Hiker 1 gets to the car at north end of section, he drives to the south end of section to pick up Hiker 2. Reasons for this: both hikers can carry day packs, they have a car to use in the evenings for going into town or to run errands, and most likely they will be able to sleep in the back of the car/truck.

Note: We met a thru-hiker who did his own type of key swap with two vehicles and just himself. He had a motorcycle and a truck – see if you can figure it out.

LASH: "Long-Ass Section Hiker," a section hiker who does long sections of the trail at a time.

LNT: "Leave No Trace," a list of principles that ask hikers to pass through the trail as though you weren't even there (don't leave any garbage, pick up after yourself, don't harm nature).

Mail drop: A method of organized resupply while hiking. This typically requires someone from home mailing packages to you according to your schedule, so you don't have to shop for groceries.

Mouse hanger: Usually seen in shelters, a cord hanging from the ceiling through a tin can with a small stick tied to the end for hikers to hang their backpacks so mice cannot get to them.

Mt. Katahdin: The northern terminus of the Appalachian Trail, located in Maine.

Nero: Short for "nearly zero" – you hike a small amount of miles that day, but take the rest of the day off.

Night hiking: Hiking at night with a headlamp.

NOBO: Northbound or north-bounder, a hiker traveling north from Springer Mountain, GA to Mt. Katahdin, ME.

Pee Rag: What some women use to dry off after urinating in the woods, usually in the form of a cotton bandana hung from the back of the pack. The sunshine dries and bleaches the bandana leaving it with no scent, and it can be thrown in the wash.

Privy: An outhouse in the woods for human waste. These will vary from bearable to "you're better off going in the woods."

PUDS: "Pointless Ups and Downs," meaning the trail will go up in elevation, then down, then up again, then down again – and repeat over and over. Hikers often feel frustrated at working so hard to go up, then to come down, and then have to go up again.

Purist: A hiker who wants to pass every single white blaze.

Resupply: To obtain more food for the next section of the trail you'll be hiking.

Ridge runner: Most likely found in high-use areas of the trail, an employee of the ATC or trail-maintaining club who educates hikers and enforces regulations. Also performs trail and shelter maintenance.

Section hiker: One who hikes the Appalachian Trail in sections (taking more than 12 months to complete the whole trail).

Shelter: 1. Your own personal place you sleep in each night (could be a tent or a hammock). 2. On the trail, a three-sided structure built with a roof, the fourth side being open to the elements, usually near a water source and a privy; sometimes called a "lean-to."

Shuttle: A ride to town or to a trail head (sometimes for a fee, sometimes included with a hostel stay).

Slack-packing: Simply put, hiking with only those things you need for the day, allowing you to carry a much smaller backpack. This can be accomplished multiple ways: someone drops you off in the morning on the trail and picks you up at night; someone drops you off in the morning and you end your hike that day at their hostel; someone drops you at trail head in the morning and meets you at end of day with your pack. The point is you have help, so you only need to carry a small daypack with water and snacks instead of a fully-weighted backpack.

SOBO: Southbound or south-bounder, a hiker traveling south from Mt. Katahdin, ME to Springer Mountain, GA.

Springer Mountain: The southern terminus of the Appalachian Trail, located in Georgia.

Stealth camping: A campsite that has been camped at before (flat areas of land for tents, usually containing a fire pit and logs), but is not in the guidebook. Also, sometimes used as a term for camping illegally.

Stile: Steps that take hikers over a fence, but livestock cannot use.

Switchback: A zig-zag trail pattern of going up a mountain, instead of going straight up - usually made to prevent erosion but is helpful for hikers as well.

Tarp: A simple piece of tent-like fabric with no door or floor.

Tent platform: A raised platform built of wood for tents to prevent erosion in that area of the woods.

Thru-hike(r): A hike or hiker of the entire Appalachian Trail within one 12-month period.

Trail angel: Someone who provides unexpected help, food, or shelter to a hiker at no cost.

Trail log or register: A notebook usually found in shelters where thru-hikers can write their thoughts or messages to other hikers. And this is where clues are found for pink or banana blazing.

Trail magic: Unexpected food or help at no cost (most welcome by thru-hikers!).

Trail name: A nickname used by a hiker. Most all section and thru-hikers have trail names. Hikers always refer to each other by trail names.

Trail town: Towns easily accessible from the Appalachian Trail, either right off the trail or a short walk or hitchhike away.

Treeline: High point of a mountain where trees stop growing due to the high elevation and climate.

Turn stile: Similar to a stile, but a zig-zag patterned structure usually with a gate that hikers can go through but livestock cannot.

Ultralight: A style of hiking that focuses on the lightest gear possible.

Vitamin I: Ibuprofen.

Widow-maker: A tree or limb that is dead but is still hanging above and could fall at any moment on your tent in the middle of the night. If it fell on a married person's tent, it could literally make someone a "widow."

Work for stay: Working for lodging instead of paying for it; usually means doing any odd jobs that the owner agrees for you to do in lieu of paying for your stay. Typically done at hostels and the White Mountain huts.

Yo-yo-ing: Term used to describe completing a thru-hike, and then turning around and completing it *again* in the other direction.

Yogi-ing: An act of "letting" food or help be offered to a thru-hiker without actually asking for it. For example, in a convenience store you are next to a person who came in with a car, and you talk loudly to your hiker friend about wishing you could get a lift back to the trail (hoping the person with the car will offer you a ride).

Zero: A day off from hiking, literally meaning

"zero" miles hiked that day.

I. KNOW BEFORE YOU GO
~ *Chica*

This seems like a given, doesn't it? Before starting any big venture, you would think one would know to do adequate research. This is not always the case.

One girl we met on the trail had no clue how to properly set up her tarp tent – and rain was expected that night. Sounds crazy, but we have to emphasize here – please investigate and study all aspects of long distance overnight hiking, and please do it *before* heading out on the trail. You will certainly learn things along the way, but a basic knowledge of your gear, your body, and everything you might encounter along the way is a must.

1. A BIT OF HISTORY

The Appalachian Trail (full name "Appalachian National Scenic Trail" and shortened as simply the "AT") is a hiking trail in the eastern United States that spans 14 states with Springer Mountain, Georgia being the terminus in the south and Mount Katahdin, Maine being the northern end.

The trail was the brainchild of forester Benton MacKaye who envisioned a cobbling of trails for overworked city folk to be able to spend time in the woods. The idea was proposed in 1921 and completed in 1936.

During that time others joined the effort to build the path. Myron Avery was the leading force of those, but he and MacKaye clashed over what the trail should be. Eventually, MacKaye bowed out and the focus shifted from MacKaye's vision of a utopian trail with work and study opportunities to a simple hiking trail.

Using a poncho instead of a tent and wearing no socks, Earl Shaffer became the first person to "thru-hike" the AT (completing the trail within a 12-month period) in 1948. It took him 124 days. At the age of 79, Shaffer repeated his feat in 1998 on the 50th anniversary of the trail. This second trip took 173 days and Shaffer complained the trail had changed and been "made too hard over the years."

The approximate 2,200-mile path (the exact mileage changes every year) that meanders through farmland, forests, and towns is maintained by 31 trail clubs and partnerships managed by The Appalachian Trail Conservancy (ATC).

For more information on the history and development of the AT, see http://www.appalachiantrail.org.

2. RESEARCH

Consider the advantage we have over those who blazed the trail before us. There is no excuse for being unprepared. Read books! It's common (and wonderful) that each year's hiking class produces a book or three. Even the worst ones can teach the prospective thru-hiker a thing or two. I didn't love every book I read in preparation for our hike, but I gleaned some valuable tips from all of them.

If reading is not your thing, watch videos on YouTube. By doing so, you will get an idea of terrain, daily schedule, mistakes, and struggles thru-hikers experience. You will get to virtually see the trail. Granted, nothing is as good as actually being on the trail, but a video is second best.

HINT: Watch our videos! We produced videos before we started the AT, gear lists before and after, daily videos while on the AT, and ongoing videos after our trek. You can find us on YouTube under "Appalachian Trail Tales."

Use the power of the internet. There are many groups and forums with experienced (and not) individuals sharing their knowledge and opinions, sometimes with a side of snark. Join AT Facebook groups and ask questions. If you're a woman, join the Appalachian Trail: Women's Group; it's a great, supportive Facebook group for women only, and unlike some of the groups out there (read: most), drama is not tolerated. Also consider creating an account on WhiteBlaze.net. WhiteBlaze has been around a long time and has threads on just about any subject related to hiking the AT. Read a few of the many blogs with information, gear reviews, and stories from the trail.

Best of all, aside from the books (try your library), all this information is free!

3. PLAN ON THE PLAN TO FAIL

Ben Franklin once said, "If you fail to plan, you are planning to fail." But remember, not only do you need a plan, but that plan needs to have a lot of flexibility built into it.

A thru-hike is a fluid thing and does not pair well with an exact schedule (I should know, being the type-A-organizer-fanatic that I am). While you may have good reasons for having a strict timeframe, such as returning to work or school, you should give yourself as much cushion time as possible.

Not allowing enough time for a thru can have two serious consequences. First of all, the pressure of a finite schedule could cause you to hike too far, too fast, resulting in a schedule-imploding injury.

Secondly, an unexpected delay (for example, a snowstorm that sends you into town for three days) derails your plans and you cannot meet your required time frame. Both of these scenarios are valid, and both could put the kibosh on a successful thru-hike.

From our training and research, I figured we could finish the trail within six months or less, but we gave ourselves an extra month to complete it. This cushion allowed for injuries or bad weather and provided the reassurance that if we took that extra month, it was OK; after all, it was in the schedule. That definitely took the pressure off us when we took three "zero" days in a row (days off from hiking) due to snow in North Carolina, or an extra zero day here or there when one of us wasn't feeling well.

The same holds true for your budget. You should plan your money budget with extra padding as well. *But, I'm excellent at hitting budgets,* you might say. OK, what happens if your tent gets ripped to shreds? Do you have several hundred dollars to buy a replacement? What if you break an arm, get Lyme disease, or need to rest in a hotel or "hostel" (dormitory-style lodging) for a day or two?

You are hiking in the wilderness everyday for 10 hours (or more) with minimal gear. It is likely that something unfortunate will happen, at least once or twice. It helps to be ready, mentally and budget-wise, to handle these bumps when they occur.

4. WHERE TO START

The actual requirement of a "thru-hike" is to hike each mile of the entire trail within one 12-month period. You can do this by going northbound (NOBO) or southbound (SOBO) the entire time.

You can also do a "flip/flop," which is any different direction scenario (*i.e.,* go north for a while then flip to the northern terminus and head south, or vice versa). Virtually any other scenario is acceptable for a flip/flop. For instance, hike one state in any direction, then skip somewhere else on the trail and hike that state in any direction, *etc.,* until you complete all 14 states.

According to the Appalachian Trail Conservancy (ATC), they are all acceptable for the thru-hiker definition, as long as you complete the entire trail within one 12-month period. In fact, due to crowding at the beginning of the NOBO season in Georgia, the ATC is encouraging prospective thru-hikers to consider alternatives to the traditional NOBO and SOBO hikes.

5. APPROACH TRAIL OR NOT

The southern terminus of the AT is at Springer Mountain, GA. One way of getting there is to actually hike the Approach Trail (8.8 miles), which is not part of the AT but leads to it. Many hikers decide to do this because it was an official part of the trail long ago or because they wish to spend the previous night at the Amicalola Lodge, as seen in the movie *A Walk in the Woods*. You may choose to take this approach so you can register at the Amicalola Falls State Park Visitor Center and weigh your pack, then start your hike at the famous archway just outside the visitor center and experience the 604 steps leading up to the gorgeous Amicalola Falls.

Another way to get to Springer Mountain is to be dropped off just north of Springer Mountain at the Springer parking area, obtainable by a dirt road – be cautious if the weather is bad. You will have to hike southbound 1.1 miles to get to Springer Mountain. Then, you will need to turn around and go north, retracing that mile you just hiked, to return to the parking lot where you will continue on the AT northbound. Yes, I know, this doesn't seem right, does it? That's just the way it is if you want to begin your hike at the official southern terminus of the trail.

Either way, you hike more than the official length of the trail (8.8 or 1.1 extra miles), but you will do this often on your thru, as you will discover.

In similar fashion, if you are hiking SOBO and starting at the summit of Mt. Katahdin, Maine (northern terminus of the AT), you must hike the 5.2 miles up Mt. Katahdin to the summit, and then back down (covering the same 5.2 miles again) and continue southbound on the AT.

We cover more details about Mt. Katahdin in Chapter VIII.

6. PERMITS/FEES

It is not necessary to register your thru-hike, but the ATC collects valuable data from the registered hikers and you get a cool plastic badge that you can hang on your backpack that shouts, "I am a registered thru-hiker!" You can register your hike online at:

http://www.appalachiantrail.org/home/explore-the-trail/thru-hiking/voluntary-thru-hiker-registration.

Permits are a different story. Three parks along the AT require permits, only one of which includes a fee.

For the NOBO hiker, The Great Smoky Mountains

National Park (GSMNP) is the first section requiring a permit and the only one requiring a fee. This comes up quickly – we arrived on Day 24. You may obtain a permit up to 30 days in advance of the date you anticipate arriving in the Smokies. The permit costs $20 and allows you eight days to get through the 71 miles of the park. We bought our permit online (https://smokiespermits.nps.gov) a couple of days before we started, as we were confident we could hike it in under 30 days; and we did, even including the Approach Trail and taking four zero days, three of which were unplanned. Another option for purchasing the permit is Fontana Village and Lodge (we stayed there the night before we started the Smokies). They have a computer and printer you can use.

Next up is Shenandoah National Park. The permit is free but must be filled out and affixed to the hiker's backpack. The form is available at a kiosk upon entering the park.

You will also need a permit in Baxter State Park where the northern terminus, Mt. Katahdin, is located. This permit is free, but paperwork must be done at the Ranger Station at Katahdin Stream Campground before summiting Mt. Katahdin.

7. TRAINING

Training your body has the same weighty importance as preparing yourself mentally. Do as much physical training as you can before your AT hike. Load your backpack with your gear so the weight is similar to what it will be on the AT, and hike with it. Go up and down stairs, or use the stair climber or treadmill on an incline at the gym. Lift weights. Do squats and lunges. Do whatever you can with the time and environment you have.

Any physical training will help, so doing any of the suggested exercises above – even on a limited basis – is better than doing nothing. Please do not stress out about not doing enough training, as there is really no way you can train adequately for being on the actual trail, day in and day out. The best training will come when you actually begin your thru-hike.

8. GEAR TEST TRIP

Because it was so helpful to us, we highly encourage you to take a "gear test trip" before you start the AT. Go on a two-three night backpack trip with all your gear. Get out there in the elements where you will have to use most of your gear. This will force you to think about everything – what works, what doesn't, and what might be missing. Hike during the day with your pack and use your trekking poles (if you plan to use them on the AT). Try to hike in the rain with your rain gear. Sleep in your shelter (tent/hammock) and try out all your clothing and cookware.

When we took our gear test trip, we hiked six miles in Devil's Lake Park in Wisconsin – over boulders and hills, around a huge lake, and in the rain, no less. At only 3:00, we were so exhausted and sore, we lay down in our tent and took a two-hour nap. And we had been training! I share this with you so you can see how green we were, but we were still able to thru-hike the whole Appalachian Trail. If we could do it – so can you!

9. NERVES

If you're nervous before you begin your first day on the trail, don't despair. Everyone else is nervous too. Don't stress about simple things like setting up your tent/hammock, finding and filtering water, or hanging your "bear bag" (bag used for food and scented items). Everyone is in the same boat (er, tent). Needing and giving help brings all the hikers together in the beginning. We were continually amazed at the kindness of people on the trail and the ease of talking and getting to know other hikers. Early on, we saw hikers showing others how to gather and filter water, how to set up a tent, how to start their stove, how to read their guidebook, *etc.*

I was so excited for the first day of our hike to arrive, but the night before we started, I suddenly broke into tears in my husband's arms! I had no idea where it came from, but I felt so emotional and could not help myself from crying. It was nerves and excitement all rolled together before starting out. We had waited so long for this day to come. All of a sudden – here we were, ready to step foot into the woods, the great and vast unknown.

II. GEARING UP
~ *Sunsets*

Equipment for a long-distance backpacking trip is a frustrating subject. It's so easy (and fun) to get bogged down in the minutia of data, and often you will spend an inordinate amount of time reading about, looking at, and trying out new gear.

Our predilection to shiny new things is ever present when researching equipment. And to a degree, it should be so. One must have specialized gear to spend six months at a time in the wilderness. While in extreme cases, the proper gear could mean the difference between life and death, more realistically it is the difference between comfortable enough and uncomfortable.

So, we concerned ourselves with getting to know materials, weights, and uses. We read reviews, asked questions on forums, and put the paraphernalia to the test.

Let's take a broad view of the gear needed for a successful Appalachian Trail hike. You will find a description of each system required for a thru-hike. We will look at specific brands or models only as examples. There are many ways to outfit your hike of the Appalachian Trail. This discussion will help.

10. EQUIPMENT SELECTION IN GENERAL

The trend today is toward super lightweight gear. The lighter the better, right? Not necessarily. Those who are trying to shave every gram from their kit are typically driven to do so because of a need for speed or a desire to have the lightest kit out there. You know, bragging rights.

But does that mean you need to cut your toothbrush in half to save a gram? Should you buy all Dynema (formerly cuben fiber) equipment? The material, used for tents, stuff sacks, and backpacks, is incredibly light for its durability but comes with a high price tag. In a word, NO. In fact, one of the most useless things I did was to cut the end off my toothbrush to save weight. The amount saved in no way offset the awkwardness and mess of brushing with a short shaft. The shortened toothbrush drove me so crazy I bought a new one before we were even out of Georgia.

The truth is, for most of us non-competitive hikers, gear choice is made by balancing a few important qualities, of which *weight* is only one. Other attributes to consider are durability, cost, multi-functionality, comfort, and warranty/customer service reputation. Keep all these things in mind as you assemble your gear, giving weight (see what I did there?) to the most important reason for that specific piece of gear.

11. GIVE ME SHELTER

There are multiple solutions to the question, "Where will I sleep on the trail?" The right one for you will depend upon several factors including: how many people will sleep in the shelter (and to some degree how tall/big they are), how many seasons the shelter will be used (a three-season shelter works best for a typical NOBO thru-hike), the level of comfort desired, weight of the shelter, and packed size.

Tents are made of several materials, but all modern lightweight tents can be categorized as being made from variants of two, either Dynema or silicon-impregnated nylon (silnylon). These two materials exhibit the properties needed for a multi-month journey: they are lightweight, waterproof and durable. Dynema is the lighter of the two materials, though its expense can be a deterrent.

The four most-used shelter systems are the tent, the tarp, the hammock, and the shelter/cowboy camp. Each has its own advantages and disadvantages.

Tent – The tent is the standard shelter and is used by most hikers on the Appalachian Trail. A tent gives the most privacy and protection from the elements.

The variety of tents on the market give the buyer many options to wade through, some of which mitigate the tent's main disadvantage, its weight.

Tents come in many configurations making the number of options either impressive or maddening based on your bent. To help you choose, consider the following factors:

How many seasons? A three-season tent will be a fine option for most NOBO thru-hikes. If you plan to hike during the winter, a four-season tent should be considered. The four-season tent will be much heavier but can shelter you from colder temps.

Dual-walled or single-walled? A single-walled tent is just that, one piece of material and nothing more. A dual-walled tent is two pieces, an interior that has mesh for airflow and a fly for rain. The dual-walled tent is heavier but can provide better ventilation resulting in a more comfortable sleep and less condensation. Also, being able to remove the rainfly on clear nights creates a sweet set-up for stargazing.

Freestanding or fixed? The next option you need to choose is whether the tent will be freestanding or not. A freestanding tent can be set up and moved and does not require stakes, although they could be added for stability when needed. A fixed tent must be staked out and cannot be moved.

Pole system or trekking pole set-up? Many tents that aim to please the ultralight backpacker do not use poles to set up the structure. Instead, the hiker uses his trekking poles for one or two of the supports. This saves weight but adds an element of risk should a trekking pole break in the field.

Tarp – Advantages to a tarp are many. They are open and allow a closer connection with nature. The structure can be set up multiple ways (based on campsite characteristics), utilizing trees or hiking poles. The tarp can be set-up at midday break for protection against sun or wind. The weight of a tarp system is minimal, especially when compared to a traditional, dual-walled silnylon tent.

One disadvantage of tarps is the openness allows access for creepy crawlies to enjoy your shelter with you. Even if your food is properly hung away from your tarp, rodents sometimes gnaw on gear to acquire nesting material.

Depending on how close to nature you want to be, there are ways to protect yourself from some of these tarp hazards. Most tarpers use a piece of Tyvek or plastic under the tarp so that the sleeping pad and other items do not touch the ground directly. Also, many will use a head bug net and/or "bivy" (bivouac sack) to protect skin from insects.

Another potential problem is water encroachment when it rains. A tent has a floor with a bathtub-like barrier rising several inches off the ground to keep water from coming into the tent. Since the tarp is open and the ground cover flat, water could be a problem. Finally, tarps take experience to set up effectively and the learning curve is steeper than that of a tent.

Hammock – Those contraptions mostly seen on an island strung between two palm trees are becoming a popular choice for the Appalachian Trail thru-hiker. Throughout the Appalachian range, lack of trees is rarely a problem; thus the trail is conducive for a hammock system. The main advantage of this suspended system is that it is easily set up in multiple spots where a traditional ground dweller will find it difficult to find a location (wet, rocky, or sloping ground). Add to that, many hikers find sleeping in a hammock to be more comfortable than sleeping on a pad on the ground.

There are a few disadvantages to the hammock system as well. First, it is a one-person-only setup. If you want to sleep next to your partner and share space at night, a tent is your best option. Secondly, generally speaking, a hammock system is going to weigh more than a tent setup. In addition to the hammock and the gear needed to attach it between trees, most people will also carry a bug net, a tarp for rain and wind protection, a top quilt for a blanket and an under quilt so heat does not escape from underneath the hammock. Finally, while there are more options of places to set up a hammock versus pitching a tent, the learning curve to be able to do so is steep.

Shelter/Cowboy Camp – A very few hardy souls (at least initially) choose not to carry a shelter with them. Rather, they make use of one of the over 250 three-sided lean-tos (also called a shelter) along the trail or they sleep under the stars. While thru-hiking without a tent, tarp, or hammock makes for a lighter pack, it can also lead to a miserable journey.

In an ideal situation, sleeping under the stars is serene; however "cowboy camping" (sleeping with no shelter) in inclement weather is uncomfortable and can be dangerous. Since a thru-hike can take six or seven months, it is certain a hiker will experience wet and cold weather.

Depending on a lean-to poses its own problems. First, shelters are not always spaced in a way convenient to your mileage itinerary. This may force you to walk an extra-long day, potentially in miserable weather, or cause you to pull up short of your desired hike distance.

Secondly, shelters do fill up and sometimes will be overflowing with dirty hikers. This is especially true when the cowboy camper is depending on them most. When it is raining or cold, even those with tents, tarps, and hammocks seek shelters to avoid the misery of setting up in bad weather.

Finally, one must consider the bugs, specifically the mosquitos and black flies that can be relentless. A tent will keep the dentist-drill drone of the ever-present mosquito at bay.

12. A THIRST FOR CLEAN WATER

A good water system will keep you walking… as opposed to running. Tainted water can cause intense stomach cramping, vomiting, and diarrhea. Two of the most common contaminates found while hiking are the protozoa *Giardia* and *Cryptosporidium*. Bacteria such as *Salmonella* and *E. coli* can be a problem as well. And finally, there are viruses to contend with.

In addition to the illness-causing bugs, water is more appetizing when it's free from "floaties"– those particles of dirt, debris, and dead things found most frequently in stagnant water, but also in moving water.

Let's look at the most common methods of handling

water on a thru-hike and the pros and cons of each.

Filters – The most common filter on the Appalachian Trail is the Sawyer Squeeze. There are other filters that do a fine job as well, but because of durability, weight, cost, and effectiveness, the Sawyer Squeeze is the go-to filter. Regardless of brand, filters will take care of protozoa and bacteria. In addition, they remove floaties and (except for tannin-tinged waters) leave water clear. The cons are few but need to be considered. Filters will not remove viruses and some filters (including the Sawyer) become useless if they freeze.

HINT: Many prospective thru-hikers begin their journey with the Sawyer Mini because it weighs a bit less than the Squeeze, only to ditch it in favor of the Squeeze for its superior flow rate.

Chemicals – Chemicals are an excellent choice. They are lightweight and take up very little room in a pack. They also take care of all four contaminants – parasites, protozoa, bacteria, and viruses.

The drawback is treated water must sit for a while for the chemicals to work, up to 20 minutes, which can be an excruciatingly long time for a thirsty hiker who carries the minimum amount of water. Also, chemicals can leave a chemical taste to the water (duh) and clearly do not remove those unappetizing floaties (ew).

Because chemicals are lightweight, they are often used as a backup should a filter fail or if a water source has been deemed unsafe because of a virus (*i.e.,* norovirus).

UV Light – These lights, of which the SteriPen is most common, disrupt the DNA of an offending bacteria, protozoa, or virus, rendering them sterile and unable to reproduce, therefore unable to cause you harm.

The UV light is lightweight and small but does have some shortfalls. You will have to first filter cloudy or highly sedimented water. Next, you will need a colored bottle, such as a Nalgene, to hold the water while you stir. Nalgenes are no longer popular among hikers due their very heavy weight. Finally, the UV light bulb could go out or break leaving the utensil useless.

Boiling – This method of water purification is extremely effective. But sadly, it is not practical for the thru-hiker. Hiking 15 to 20 miles a day requires many liters of water. In fair weather on our thru, we consumed about one liter per five miles. In humid and hot conditions, this doubled. Since water is heavy (2.2 pounds per liter, not including the receptacle), you will need to carry one to two liters at a time. So, every couple of hours, you will need to gather and purify water. Boiling water not only takes time, but requires fuel, which is also heavy. For these reasons boiling water as a stand-alone purification strategy is not a good option. We never saw anyone use this method.

Water Roulette – Some hikers refuse to treat water. Maybe they feel more manly or closer to nature or just plain brave. Their strategy is to gather water from the most reliable sources, springs or streams not far from a spring source. The problem with this strategy is a spring is not always available. You will eventually need to gather water from a river or even a lake.

You have no good reason not to be safe. Carry the extra three ounces for a filter or the almost nothing weight of a chemical treatment. Let's be honest: you are going to lose weight on your thru because you can't get enough calories. No sense in adding to your weight loss by contracting a (preventable) stomach bug.

13. BACKPACK

You have all this gear, so how are you going to carry it all and keep it dry and organized? In a backpack, of course. A great pack will distribute the 25-35 pounds the typical hiker carries on the hipbones, saving the back and shoulders from strain.

While backpacks come in a multitude of sizes (denoted in liters of volume), the thru-hiker usually ends up with a backpack between 45 and 65 liters. In addition to volume, packs come in various sizes to fit multiple body shapes and have belts that fit a variety of girths.

Fit is important, especially for the thru-hiker who will depend on the pack for many months. Torso length and how the hip belt sits on the hipbones are the two main areas of concentration when fitting a backpack.

There are three main types of backpacks to consider.

Frameless – The champion of the ultralight hiker and the bane of everyone else. The popularity of these packs has soared, but they are designed for lower total weights, usually less than 25 pounds. When employed by those carrying more than that, pain often ensues.

The main benefit of the frameless pack is it can be pounds lighter than its internal frame counterparts.

External Frame – These backpacks have a tubular metal frame on the outside. They are designed for carrying heavy loads, but are rarely seen in use by thru-hikers these days. For an example of the external framed backpack, watch the movie *Wild*. Reese Witherspoon's character carries a load of about 70 pounds in an external frame backpack, rightfully nicknamed "Monster."

Internal Frame – The happy median between the frameless and external extremes. As the name implies the frame is hidden inside the pack. The internal frame is widely used by thru-hikers for many reasons (Osprey backpacks being a favorite). They can carry a heavy load, have multiple organizing pockets, and provide suspension and support, while being lighter and more streamlined than an external frame.

14. FOOD FOR THOUGHT

When thru-hiking you typically burn more calories than you can possibly consume. Therefore, it behooves you to keep your food safe from pests, such as bears, rodents, and raccoons. Below are the main ways hikers secure their food.

Bear Bag – A bear bag is typically a waterproof food bag with a capacity between 8-20 liters that folds and secures at the opening. The size you choose would depend on the number of days you plan to hike before resupplying. With a carabiner and bear-line, it can be hung over a tree branch at a height where bears cannot reach it. Bear bags are usually made of Dyneema or some version of silnylon, so they are waterproof. The bag can be hung in various ways with the Pacific Crest Trail (PCT) method ironically being preferred on the Appalachian Trail.

The Ursack – This specialized food bag, made from Kevlar, is designed to withstand violent investigations by bears. The bag typically is not hung; rather, it is tied to a tree to keep a bear from easily carrying it away.

We met a couple who were each using an Ursack for their food. One night, a bear came into camp and both Ursacks failed against the claws of their namesake, *Ursus americanus*, the black bear. The company replaced both bags for having a manufacturing defect. Obviously, the couple needed to hang a bag in the interim, and they chose to purchase a traditional bear bag.

I don't tell you this story to deter you from considering the Ursack; the same stories can be told of poorly hung traditional bear bags. But it is a reminder that gear and systems can fail on the trail and you need to be prepared.

Bear Canister – A bear canister is exactly what the name implies; it is a small barrel with a screw top lid that secures food. The canister is not hung, but is typically wedged under a fallen tree to give the prospective food thief a bit of a challenge. Even if the bear pries the bucket from its hiding place, the receptacle is strong enough to withstand the attack.

There are three main disadvantages to the bear canister. First, being made of hard plastic, they are a fixed size and will not fit in some backpacks, though they can be lashed to the outside. Secondly, they are much heavier than the bear bag counterparts. Furthermore, if a bear is interested in the canister, even if he cannot get at the food, he can bat the barrel far from where you secured it, and it may be difficult, if not impossible, to find.

Currently, one section on the Appalachian Trail requires a bear canister. It is not a long section, and if you are not staying overnight in the designated area, you don't need to carry one. Check with the Appalachian Trail Conservancy for canister regulations for the year you hike.

Bear Bait – The easiest (and laziest and stupidest) system of all is to do nothing but keep your food in your tent. What's the worst that could happen? The internet is filled with anecdotes of backpackers never securing their food and never having a problem. Ever. For a whole thru-hike. Right?

There are just as many stories of campers leaving one empty candy wrapper in the tent and waking to a tsunami of claws ripping through the thin tent material they thought would protect them from the wild outside.

I don't know about you, but I choose to protect myself and my food.

15. COOK SYSTEM

Cook Pot – Cook pots are typically made of aluminum or the lighter, more expensive titanium. Most hikers find the 700ml or 900ml size to be sufficient. Make sure the pot has a lid; food will cook faster. I prefer plastic-coated handles which are not too hot to touch while using.

Chica's pot did not have plastic coated handles, but we were able to buy tubing at our local hardware store to affix to the handles and melt into place. More trouble than necessary if you ask me.

Cook Stove – While there may be some chefs or cooking enthusiasts on the trail, most thru-hikers want to cook, do their evening chores, and get to bed as quickly as possible. In other words, they need a stove only to boil water, the faster the better. Boiled water is added to pasta and rice sides, to mac and cheese, and to instant mashed potatoes, all staples of thru-hiker dinners and all made simply with boiling water. For coffee and tea on cool mornings, again, you only need hot water.

Heating water by a campfire is not practical for daily use, so a stove is in order. The three most common types seen on the trail are: lightweight stoves (MSR Pocket Rocket), the all-in-one stove and cup (Jetboil), and the homemade alcohol stove. The first two use a gas canister which is easily found everywhere along the trail. The third stove is made from an aluminum soda can or cat food container and uses liquid fuel, like Heet or denatured alcohol that is poured directly into the container. The fuel for this type of stove is also found readily along the trail; however, it requires a container and can be messy, but you can save weight by buying the exact amount you need.

Spork – Spork is a portmanteau that combines the words spoon and fork. These can be plastic or metal and short or long-handled. The long handle is great for digging into a deep jar of food, such as peanut butter, and getting every morsel.

Titanium and aluminum are preferable to plastic as they are more likely to last the entire thru-hike.

Going Cold – Most hikers start with a cook system. A hot meal at the end of a cold day or cup of joe on a frigid morning helps morale, and having a stove and cook pot in such conditions may even save you from hypothermia. However, once summer hits, some hikers send their cookware home and eat uncooked food. This might be jerky, or packs of tuna and crackers. Some even soak noodles in cold water and eat them cold. The logic here is hot food is unappetizing in hot weather, and some weight can be saved by sending the cook stove home.

We sent our stove home right around the halfway point and never regretted not having it. We decided to send it home because we did not want to fire it up and clean up every night; besides, we were already eating cold food. We would have dinners of jerky, cheese, crackers, tortillas, and peanut butter. Occasionally we would pack a sandwich or other premade foods from a deli or grocery store.

16. SLEEP SYSTEM

On a thru-hike you are going to put your body through physical stress it has most likely never experienced before. And you are going to do this day in and day out for 8, 10, or 12 hours a day, for half a year. You need to be able to recover and a good sleep will do wonders for your body. Let's look at the gear you need.

Sleeping Pad – Sleeping pads not only add comfort,

buffering you from the hard ground, but they also provide insulating properties, so body heat is not lost to the ground, letting you sleep warm and safe.

Sleeping pads come in two varieties, both of which are widely used on thru-hikes. The first is a closed-cell foam pad, which folds up like an accordion. Because they are made of foam, they cannot be punctured or deflated. They are lightweight and durable, although most find them less comfortable than an inflatable mattress.

The second type of pad is the air mattress, which provides a more comfortable sleep. The downsides are they can be punctured so you have to carry a repair kit, they can be loud when a sleeper moves around, and they must be inflated. This last point doesn't sound awful on the surface, but 30 big breaths after a long day of putting in miles drives some people mad.

Sleeping Bag/Quilt – A traditional mummy bag cocoons the sleeper, and the zipper closes the hiker in all the way up to his chin. A quilt, on the other hand, is open with only a zippered section at the bottom to create a footbox. The rationale is straightforward: since bodyweight crushes the down between the body and the ground, eliminating most of its insulating properties, the quilt removes this section. This saves weight and cost and doesn't affect warmth or comfort.

Both options have their adherents. Both come in multiple sizes (length and width) and both come in various degree ratings. The degree ratings are given by manufactures and typically denote the temperature which the bag/quilt will keep you alive, rather than comfortable. For the hiker wanting one bag for the entire thru-hike, most will go with a 10 or 20-degree bag and carry an optional sleeping bag liner, which can add 10-15 degrees of warmth in the colder months. Or they will sleep only with the liner in summer and send their bag/quilt home.

In addition, if you are hammocking, you will need to purchase an underquilt to protect against heat loss, just as a hiker who pitches a tent would use a sleeping pad.

Pillow – Pillows come in many varieties. For the ultralight backpacker, a puffy jacket folded into its own pocket is plenty, or maybe a clothing-filled stuff sack with a "buff" (bandana-like cloth typically worn on the head) wrapped around it. For the hiker willing to give up two or three ounces and $20, a cloudlike inflatable pillow can feel like a real luxury on the trail.

17. RAIN, RAIN, GO AWAY

Any rain system you choose is going to suck. There, I said it. It's a truth not many want to talk about. Many hikers devolve in warmer weather and choose to be wet with rain instead of sweat because the word "breathable" doesn't mean to clothing companies what it does to us.

Still, being drenched is miserable and, in some conditions, can cause hypothermia. Therefore, we must address the topic of rain gear to stay reasonably comfortable and safe.

Poncho – A rain poncho is a waterproof garment that envelopes the top half of the wearer's body. Imagine a plastic sheet with a hole cut in the center for your head to fit through, add a hood, and you've got a pretty close estimation of what a poncho is.

There are many reasons why a poncho is a wise choice for a thru-hike. First, because they are open at the sides, airflow is much greater compared to a rain jacket. The poncho is inexpensive and made from thin material and is light to carry. You can also get one large enough to fit over your backpack so that even the straps are covered. The problem then is the poncho will billow up in even the slightest wind. Tie a piece of paracord as a belt and the problem is averted. Finally, a poncho can serve as a groundcover to sit on and, if large enough, even as a tarp shelter.

For all their benefits, ponchos do have a downside. They are bulky when worn and, even though a thru-hike is not a fashion show, they look ridiculous. Clearly a situation of function over fashion.

Skirt/Kilt – Think of a rain skirt as a poncho for your lower body. I used a rain skirt for the entire trip and loved it. I got it from ULA Equipment and liked the ability to control airflow while keeping my shorts dry. Like the poncho, the skirt can be used to drape over a wet log you want to sit on or as a ground cover to lay out gear. We used this regularly for breaks during our thru.

Jacket and Pants – The combination of rain pants paired with a jacket is the traditional approach to keeping dry. The combo can be inexpensive but heavy, like Frogg Toggs, or expensive and made with the latest in technologically advanced (but still stifling) materials. Jacket and pants are the most common solution for the rain problem if only because they are the most familiar to new hikers.

Breathability is always a problem, but of all the options, this combo is the most restrictive of airflow. Jackets often have "pit zips" that can be zipped open for breathability, but there is nothing that can be done with the pants. You will be working, lumbering up and down mountains, and you will sweat. The question for you is, will you be more uncomfortable sweating or getting rained on?

Umbrella – Chica used an umbrella with success. She would thread the handle through her backpack chest-strap and secure it with her hip-belt, leaving both hands free so she could use her trekking poles. For her, keeping the rain off her head and off the top of her backpack, helped her feel more comfortable while hiking in the uncomfortable. The umbrella was also useful when we were in town.

Keeping Backpack Contents Dry – Keeping the contents of your backpack dry is a must. Down-filled items, like your puffy jacket and sleeping bags, are useless wet. Even if the dampness doesn't affect an item's usefulness, wet gear is annoying.

Multiple products, used individually or in combination, are available to protect the contents of a backpack: stuff sacks, pack rain covers, and trash compactor bags to line the pack.

For the interior, many choose to organize and protect their clothing with a waterproof stuff sack. Stuff sacks also allow the hiker to group items and control weight distribution in the pack. Another internal protection is a plastic trash compactor bag. These bags are designed for kitchen compactors and can withstand the daily abuse of taking gear out at night and repacking in the morning.

HINT: If you use this method to protect your gear, buy a white bag instead of black so you will be able to see your gear better when you look into your bag.

Finally, backpackers often want to protect the outside of their packs. Most packs are water resistant but will eventually allow water to soak through and this can reach the contents of your pack. A pack cover can minimize this. A water-logged pack is heavy, much heavier than a cover that only weighs an ounce or two. Also, the pack cover can help keep your pack clean when you take it off and set it down in muddy conditions, and it can protect the pack when walking through heavy brush.

We used all three methods to keep our stuff dry. Overkill? Maybe, but our gear stayed dry and the weight for the cover, compactor bag, and stuff sacks was minimal.

18. CLOTHING SYSTEM

Using a layering system on your thru-hike will ensure maximum comfort and minimal danger of exposure. The following typical layers, combined and added to a rain system, allow for success in almost any weather you may experience. Obviously, if you are SOBO and/or hiking during winter months, your clothing and shelter gear will need to keep you safe in colder conditions.

Many NOBO hikers send cold weather gear home for the summer. Some use Damascus, Virginia for this purpose, while others wait a bit longer until they summit Mount Rogers, Virginia's tallest peak on the Appalachian Trail. The NOBO hiker typically retrieves cold weather gear starting around Hanover, NH, but certainly before reaching the White Mountains in New Hampshire.

Base Layer – A base layer is typically two pieces of clothing each for upper body and lower body. The purpose of the base layer is to wick moisture to keep the skin dry. The base layer is typically snug and made from merino wool or a synthetic blend. Hikers pack base layers in both short and long versions to accommodate multiple temperature ranges.

An example base layer packing list for a thru-hiker in the cooler months might include these four items: merino wool t-shirt, merino wool long-sleeved midweight shirt, lined running shorts (or underwear under normal shorts), and synthetic running tights for use under the shorts.

Insulating Layer – This layer traps the heat and keeps you warm. Examples of the insulating layer are fleece jackets and puffy jackets. Hikers often prefer down-filled puffy jackets because they can be packed down into a very small package (often into their own pocket), and they are incredibly light for their warming power.

Gloves and Cap – Another necessity in colder climates is the cap-and-gloves combo. Gloves help keep your hands warm and dry while the cap does the same for your head and ears. Material is typically wool or fleece.

19. FOOTWEAR

The two main options when it comes to footwear are boots and trail runners. You may hear of hikers called *Sandals,* who earned their "trail name" (hiker nickname) by hiking the trail in Tevas; and yes, there are even those who hike barefoot... or at least they start out that way. For most of us though, we require a bit more foot protection from the constant assault of rocks and roots.

Boots – The old standby, leather boots, used to be the only thing anyone would consider hiking in. Boots wear down slowly, provide ankle support and are, in a word, bombproof. They also require a long break-in period, are heavy and more apt to cause blisters, and take a long time to dry out when saturated.

Now, hybrid boots provide ankle support, like their leather counterparts, but are made of quicker-drying material. These are a great choice for those hikers who need the support of a boot but want a lighter option that will dry out faster.

Trail Runners – Many long-distance hikers are coming around to the benefits of hiking in shoes designed for trail running. They are light and fast-drying and have an aggressive enough tread for most of the hiking terrain one will experience on the trail.

Trail runners do fail in a couple of areas as well. They provide little ankle support, they wear out much quicker than traditional boots, and for those who are carrying heavier loads, they may not be practical.

Socks – Merino wool is a magical material that wicks sweat, sheds water, cools skin or retains heat as needed. It is almost unanimous; socks made of merino wool are the best for hiking. Darn Tough and Smartwool are two popular brands used on the trail.

20. GUIDES

Even though the trail has "white blazes" (2" x 6"

swatches of white paint on trees, posts and rocks) to show the way of the trail, we highly recommend having a guidebook as well. It helps you to see what's ahead, what the elevation coming up is like and where the next "trail town" is (a town easily accessibly from the AT). A guide should also include maps with hostels, hotels, stores, amenities, and many other things.

The Appalachian Trail Thru-Hiker's Companion (by the Appalachian Long Distance Hikers Association) is the official guidebook and is regularly updated, but *The AT Guide* by David "Awol" Miller (Awol's *Guide*) is the most popular guide used on the trail. It is also published each year, and you can buy as "northbound" or "southbound" and as a bound book, loose leaf or pdf. His website (https://theatguide.com) also has paper maps of the AT available for purchase.

HINT: If you buy the guide on his website (vs. Amazon), you will get a handy heavy-duty ziplock bag to keep it dry.

To save weight, some hikers use only a section of Awol's *Guide* at a time, but we wanted to keep the whole book with us for our hike so Chica could doodle and take notes in it. If you want to keep the whole guide for your entire thru, order the bound version, but then take it to a print shop and have them spiral bind it for you. We did this and it worked great. We could easily keep it opened to the page we were on and write in it. If you want to use only a few pages at a time, order the loose leaf book. It works well, but don't expect to take this somewhere and have it spiral bound as there is not enough room at the top of pages to do this.

There is an app for smartphones called *Guthook's Appalachian Trail*, cost of $59.99 (at time of this publication) for the whole trail. It is broken down into segments, so you don't have the whole app loaded to your phone at once, and is GPS based. A common concern is *will this drain my phone battery?* It does not! Nor does it use wifi or cell data. We kept our phone in airplane mode the entire time and used Guthook's flawlessly. It always knew where we were on the trail, and more importantly, calculated how many miles we had left to camp each night.

21. LUXURY ITEMS

Luxury items are those things you want but don't need on a hike. Some examples might be an inflatable pillow to sleep on instead of your clothing stuff sack, a deck of playing cards, an e-reader, or a flask filled with your favorite booze. Hikers generally think critically before choosing luxury items because they can bloat pack size and add weight. However, what you think is unnecessary may be the thing that ensures your five to seven months on the trail are bearable. A little luxury may be obligatory.

******

Building your thru-hike gear kit can seem a daunting task. To help you see what it looks like when it is all together, we have added our gear list, as well as those of some of our friends, to the bonus section at the end of this book. You can see there are many ways to outfit an Appalachian Trail thru-hike. We chose our gear based on some measure of each of the criteria mentioned in the beginning of this chapter: durability, utility, cost, weight, and comfort.

III. MONEY, MONEY, MONEY
~ **Chica**

Unless you have been multi-day hiking for years, you will need to purchase some or possibly all of the necessary gear for your thru-hike. Between buying gear before the trail and staying and resupplying in town while on the trail, you will need to spend some cash.

Running out of money is one of the top contenders for why thru-hikers quit. Don't want this to happen to you? Plan ahead and budget. When we were doing research for our thru-hike, we could not find any summarized information on costs. Sure, we found individual prices of typical food resupply, hostel and hotel prices, but there was no total daily/weekly summary of what a typical thru-hiker might spend... until now.

22. WATCH OUR WEEKLY MONEY UPDATE VIDEOS

We decided to do our own "Weekly Update" video reports from the trail that lay out exactly what we spent each week. You can find these on YouTube under "Appalachian Trail Tales" (there is a separate playlist for it). Remember, we hiked as a couple, and probably spent more than the average thru-hiker as we wanted to have a "comfortable" thru-hike, but at least this will give you a starting place to start planning your budget. You can see what we spent and know you can save money by going cheaper or have a more luxurious hike by budgeting more money. The last "Weekly Update" video encompasses our whole time on the AT with totals of money spent on our whole hike.

With guesstimating how long it will take you to thru-hike, plus how much you plan to spend each week (including zero days), you will have your budget. It's as simple as that. Also, you now have a reason NOT to quit – you already have your spending planned and the money set aside.

23. SPREADSHEETS

Spreadsheets are your friend. Almost every type of computer or laptop has some type of spreadsheet program these days. Even if you've never used a spreadsheet, it's pretty easy to figure out. Just start inputting information into the rows and columns, and you can easily search online for simple tutorials on how to sum up several cells (or do almost any type of equation you want). You can also play with the size of the cells, put borders or boxes around items, and highlight or change the size or color of the font.

I love making and playing around with spreadsheets

(can you tell?), so this was my job before we left for the trail. I had a budget spreadsheet, a mileage spreadsheet, a gear list (with weights) spreadsheet, a spreadsheet for where people wanted to meet us or send us care packages… you get the drift. Even if you don't follow the spreadsheets exactly, they will definitely help you plan, budget, and stay organized for your thru.

24. WHAT'S IN YOUR WALLET?

One thing a thru-hike will teach you is you really don't need much to live on for five-seven months in the woods. Instead of a large purse, all I carried was a 3" x 4" waterproof wallet from Zpacks.com. Sunsets had the same in a different color. This is big enough to hold a few cards and some cash and has a nice loop on one end to attach inside your pack. We both carried three cards (driver's license, debit card, credit card) and some cash, which all fit perfectly. The credit card was for emergencies but we never used it. The cash was for hostels, shuttles and tips. Some hostels will only take cash; Awol's *Guide* will most likely mention this, but not every time, so always ask when you're calling to make a reservation. Also, there's nothing worse than coming across a vending machine with ice-cold sodas on a hot day but not having any cash on you.

25. SEPARATE ACCOUNT

Think about a separate checking account with debit card for your thru-hike expenses. We were able to set this up at no cost with our bank. This account was separate but tied to our main checking account, so if we needed to transfer money over to it, we could easily do so online. The best part for me was it kept our AT money separate for budgeting purposes. It also protects your main account should the card for your secondary account become lost or stolen.

26. DEBIT CARD TIP

Use your debit card at the grocery store and take money out at the register to avoid ATM fees. This saved us so many times! ATMs are a-plenty, but your specific bank's ATM? Not so much. Unless you can find your bank's ATM, you will usually pay a fee. Some excellent banks will reimburse you (I've heard Charles Schwabb, for one), but most banks do not.

It's so easy to take some cash out after you pay for your groceries at the grocery store. You usually have the option to take out $20, $40, $60, $80 or $100 at a time.

27. CASH IS KING (SOMETIMES)

Always ask if there is a discount for paying in cash. One time we were able to save 20% at a hotel! It may be easier to use a credit or debit card, but if your goal is to save money, ask. Most hostels will typically have a cash discount and some will only take cash, so please be prepared or call ahead to find out.

28. DISCOUNT CARDS

Before you start your hike, obtain membership/discount cards for any stores that require them for a discount. We found cards necessary at CVS Pharmacy and Ingels Markets to name a couple, and the cards saved us money as well. If you don't have a card and don't want to register for one, ask the clerk if they have a general one for this purpose. Sometimes they'll even use their own card. People will surprise you with how helpful they are, especially when they hear you are thru-hiking the Appalachian Trail.

29. CAMP OUTSIDE OF TOWN

If you want access to the amenities in town without paying for a hotel, you can camp for free just outside of town. Sometimes there are even places in town that offer free tenting (or for a nominal fee, like at hostels). You can do this at select places along the AT; refer to Awol's *Guide* for showers, laundry and resupply icons on the town maps.

When we were thru-hiking, we came into the NOC (Nantahala Outdoor Center) at mid-day and ran into friends who told us about the place where they camped the night before – behind the NOC and down the railroad tracks a bit, right beside a lovely river. We hadn't planned to stay there, but we still had a nine-mile climb out of the NOC, so we decided to check out this spot. It was perfect, so we set up our tent and went back into town for dinner. We found bathrooms, coin-showers and a coin-laundry nearby – all the amenities of a hostel without the overnight fee. And camping in our tent next to a roaring river, we had the best night's sleep ever!

A couple of other places that stand out in my mind that make it easy to camp outside of town are Fontana Hilton Shelter/Fontana Village, NC and Boiling Springs, PA.

30. NERO INSTEAD OF ZERO

A "zero" day is when you take a day off from hiking, which can entail paying for a hotel/hostel for two nights when you choose to take your breaks in town. A "nero" is a nearly zero day, meaning you hike for a small part of the day but take the rest of the day off. After we got further into our hike, we started doing neros instead of zeros. Why? Because with a full zero day, you need to pay for a night's stay for two nights, but with a nero, only one night is required. Also a nero means less time in town and less going out for meals. A full zero day was almost too much time off the trail, and we found ourselves getting restless and ready to be back on the trail.

We finally figured out that a nero was all we needed on town days. A nero enabled us to get some hiking in (early morning we would hike 6-11 miles into town), hopefully check in somewhere early (almost *all* hotels and hostels allowed this for thru-hikers), shower, eat, do laundry, and relax for the rest of the day with a good night's sleep in a bed. By the next morning, we were totally refreshed and ready to start hiking again.

31. KEEP DRINKS TO A MINIMUM

Hikers like to party and drink quite a bit of alcohol while they are in town. Hey, it does help the aching feet. However, alcohol in restaurants or bars can totally drain your savings. If you drink, try buying whatever your prefer at the grocery or convenience store and drink in your hotel room or hostel instead, if allowed. We found that a six-pack of beer in the store was the same price as two beers at a restaurant/bar.

32. THREESOMES

If you are in a group of two or more, a hotel room will probably be cheaper than a hostel, even if they charge you an extra fee per person. We saw groups of three or four hikers in a two-bed hotel room all the time, even some that just met the same day on the trail. Even we, as a married couple, shared a hotel room with another person a few times. Some things that seem very odd in every day life are common on the trail and in the thru-hiker community.

33. GROUP DISCOUNTS

Ask for group discounts for shuttle rides and "slack-packing" (hiking with only a daypack). You might need a shuttle from the trail to a hostel, from town back to the trail, up or down the trail (slack-packing), or into town from the hostel for resupply or going out to eat. Slack-packers hand off all or most of their backpack to another person for the day. Without the load of your full pack weight, you can conceivably hike more miles at a faster rate. You might use only a small daypack to carry a few essentials (water filter, snacks, first aid, rain coat, *etc.*). You can either retrieve your full pack at a road crossing or parking lot later in the day (to camp out in the woods) or be driven to a hostel for the night.

Almost all places we asked had a group discount for shuttling and slack-packing, and we certainly took advantage of this in southern Maine towards the end of our hike. The weather had turned chilly, I was coming down with a cold, and we were getting emotionally tired. Slack-packing helped give us that lift we needed (we may or may not have slack-packed for eight days straight at one point!). Having no weighted packs on our backs made us feel like we were flying and we hiked so much faster without them.

34. DOLLAR STORE RESUPPLY

"Resupplying" is defined as obtaining your food supply for the next amount of days that you'll be on the trail/in the woods. You can resupply while in a trail town by either shopping or having a resupply box sent to you from home.

When resupply shopping and trying to save money, if you have the choice, first choose dollar stores. We, and our hiker friends, were impressed that we could find everything we needed for a resupply at dollar stores, and it was so much cheaper than a grocery store, gas station, or even Walmart. Walmart was a great second choice, as the selection is huge and the prices affordable. Grocery stores would be next in line and convenience stores last (poor selection and usually higher prices).

35. RESUPPLY ONLINE

One guy we met on the trail, in order to save money, ordered his resupply online from Walmart.com. He made sure he ordered over a certain amount so that he got free shipping and had it sent ahead to the next trail town he would stop in. We compared prices with him, and he was certainly saving more money than we were. However, this does take some planning and meeting your schedule, which sounds easier than it is.

Planning where you'll be in the next few days is hard, the next week or two even harder. Depending on people you are hiking with, weather, and difficulty of the trail, you don't know for sure how far you will hike each day.

If sending something to a town's post office, be aware of the hours. They are almost always closed on Sundays and only open for mornings or not at all on Saturdays, and sometimes are closed over lunch on the weekdays. You'd think it would be easy to work around this, but it is surprisingly not. I can't tell you how many times we planned and planned, and *still* got to town right after the post office closed. Refer to Awol's *Guide* for post office hours.

36. WORK FOR STAY

Work for stay can take place at a hostel or "hut" (log cabins along the AT in the White Mountains of New Hampshire, where day/section/thru-hikers can make reservations to stay for a fee). Work for stay allows a hiker to work in lieu of paying for a night's stay. You'll have to do whatever is needed at the time, which you can work out with the owner/manager. This may mean washing dishes, stripping beds and doing laundry, cleaning the bathroom, *etc.* It could be anything. It is always acceptable to ask a hostel owner if work for stay is an option. The White's huts always have work for stay for hikers, but you have to get there at a certain time to be allowed to sign up for it (more information on this in Chapter VIII.).

37. DEALS

Keep your eyes and ears open for thru-hiker-specific deals at all times. Here's an example: when we were in Manchester Center, VT, we went to the laundromat. We were freshly showered and in our clean town clothes. Another hiker friend was there, fresh from the trail, and told us to ask at the service desk for free laundry soap for hikers. We were not aware of that option and the attendant would certainly not have told us because we looked squeaky clean. Sure enough, they asked us if we were thru-hikers, and then gave us free laundry soap and a dryer sheet.

Speaking of laundromats, another way to save money is to go in on a load of laundry with two or three other hikers. Usually the amount of clothes that a hiker has is pretty minimal, and three hikers can make up one load's worth. Sharing the load saves you money on the washers, dryers and soap.

Besides deals, you will soon find that people are generally quite gracious and giving towards thru-hikers. One morning as we were leaving town, there were no other food or coffee shops in the area, and right before we reached the trail entrance, we spotted a mechanic's shop. We stopped in to see if they had coffee for sale. They did have coffee but would not accept any money from us! We chatted for a bit, they wished us well on our journey, and we left with two large steaming coffees. What a great start to our day.

38. SOCIAL MEDIA

When you meet other hikers, it's a good idea to follow them/friend them on social media, even if you don't know them well. Why? Of course you might want to keep in touch with them and you don't know when you'll see them again. But here's the money saving reason: IF by chance they get ahead of you, you will have *real time tips* from someone who is just ahead of you on the trail. This is great for closures, fires, new hostels that just opened, "trail magic" (unexpected food or help at no cost), cool campsites, swimming holes, free shuttles – anything that's going on in real time that the guidebook wouldn't necessarily know about. Also, you can message them and ask their advice for a place to stay if you're not sure where to stay in the next town.

And don't forget to pass on information to the people following you!

IV. SHELTER ME
~ *Sunsets*

Each day on an Appalachian Trail thru-hike, a hiker has multiple experiences. You witness the awe of nature, persevere through adversity, and endure extreme fatigue. You sweat, you struggle, you swear, and at the end of a tough day of climbing, nothing is more important than having a place to lay your head and recuperate. Knowing how to find shelter is imperative, and so is knowing how to act when you get there.

39. GENERAL ETIQUETTE

It may come as a shock to have a tip about shelter/hostel decorum. I mean, we are all out in the middle of the forest partly to get away from societal impositions, including people telling us what to do. While true, it is also true that on the Appalachian Trail, especially in the evenings, resources are going to be shared by a diverse group of people and being conscientious and considerate can go a long way in helping everyone get along.

One of the first concepts to understand is "hiker midnight." While more an observance than a rule, most hikers are tired from a day of ups and downs, therefore the level of noise and lights at a shelter/hostel typically dims around 9 p.m., hiker midnight.

Speaking of lights, when using your headlamp to read or to mill about a shelter or campsite, please use the red-light mode. You will still be able to see, and so will your campmates, as they won't be blinded by the white light.

Sadly, I must spell it out, but if you have found love on the trail, a full shelter or the top bunk at a hostel is not the place to have your amorous tryst. Get a private room or find a bathroom with a locking door, please.

And while we are on the subject of messes, your mom is not on the AT with you. Okay, she might be, but you get the figure of speech. If you use a dish in a hostel, wash it. If you spill something, wipe it up. If you are in shared and confined quarters, either a shelter or hostel, gear explosions (when you spread your gear about) are discouraged.

Shelters are more social accommodations than are tent sites along the Appalachian Trail. If you want solitude, it's best to find a tent spot away from the shelter. This doesn't mean the shelter is a free-for-all. Smokers (of all varieties) should ask shelter-mates if it's okay to smoke at the shelter and be prepared to smoke away from it if it will disturb other occupants. Hikers smoking marijuana or drinking heavily should make sure there are no children present, and if there are, they should take the party away from the shelter.

A lean-to can be a necessity for avoiding dangerous hypothermia in cold and wet conditions. That means occupancy of shelters will swell. Safety trumps comfort and personal space in this scenario, and room should be made for newcomers until absolutely no more room is available.

If you are hiking with a pet and staying at a shelter, remember human needs come before the animal's and if there is no room, or if a shelter-mate objects, the pet will need to sleep outside the shelter.

And finally, nobody likes your music selection as much as you do. Seriously. Use headphones.

Headphones are also a good idea if you have your phone's alarm clock set to go off the next morning (so you don't wake the whole shelter or hostel).

Thru-hikers tend to understand these social manners and most of the time those individuals who are inconsiderate are out only for the day or a holiday weekend. Therefore, most problems you experience will be at shelters closest to a road or park.

Enough with the suggested rules. Let's talk about some tips for getting the most out of tent sites, hostels, and shelters.

40. STEALTH/TENT SITE TIPS

Many thru-hikers want solitude. They don't want to deal with sleeping next to someone or listening to someone snore all night. These hikers usually tent/hammock in the woods instead of staying in the shelters.

Those who want to get far away find a stealth campsite. People quibble about the definition of stealth camping, but we use the term in this book to mean any non-published or unofficial campsite. Below are five things to watch out for when choosing the ideal spot to pitch your tent.

The first and most important thing to do? Look up! "Widow-makers" are dead limbs in a tree that, if they fell, could cause serious harm to the sleeping campers or destroy the tent. They are common, so make it a habit to look for them before you begin setting up.

Flat, previously used sites are ideal and since they already exist, they adhere to the LNT (leave no trace) principles. The ideal spot is rock and root-free and not on a slope. If you pitch it on a slope, gravity will force you against one of the walls of your tent. It's not a fun way to sleep. Also, an overall hump in the tent footprint is preferable to a depression, especially if rain is in the forecast, since water can pool in the depression.

In a perfect world, tent sites should be 200 feet from the trail and water source. The AT corridor is not a perfect world and you will find many sites, stealth and shelter, that disregard the 200-foot guideline. Still, consideration should be given especially around water sources. Sleeping next to a babbling brook seems idyllic, but by doing so you could foul the water, ruining the source for others. In addition, mosquito, bug, and wildlife traffic increases around water.

For obvious reasons, your site should be as far from and upwind of a "privy" (a primitive outhouse in the woods) as possible.

Finally, amenities, either naturally occurring or those left by other campers, can make a sloping, root-filled tent site more bearable by making camp life easier or more pleasant. They could include a fire ring, logs to sit on, easy bear bag hanging branches, easily accessible cold spring, *etc.* Official shelters are going to have the most amenities, including bear cables, bear boxes, or bear poles to make it easy to secure your food. Also, shelters almost always have tenting areas, a water source nearby, and a privy.

41. PLATFORM TENTING TIPS

The NOBO hiker becomes accustomed to setting up their tent by staking it to the ground. As they move further north, however, they begin seeing more and more tent platforms. They look like a backyard deck – a square or rectangular platform made from 2x4's or 2x6's designed to hold one or more tents. If you are not prepared, it might be confusing to secure your tent to the platform.

Most platforms will have eye screws or nails in place so that you can tie your guy lines. It helps to have extra paracord so that you can reach the tie downs. It also helps to attach a carabiner to the eye screw and use line locks for each of your guy lines. This way you can run multiple guy lines to the same eye hook.

On bigger platforms you may only be able to tie out three sides. In this case on the fourth side, you can wedge a stake between the slats of the platform.

You may have to get creative, especially with non-freestanding tents that require multiple stakes.

42. SHELTER TIPS

Over 250 three-sided structures along the

Appalachian Trail are designed to house anywhere from four to twenty weary hikers. They operate on a first-come, first-served basis and not only provide a dry place to sleep, but they reduce the impact of hikers on the trail.

In addition to the etiquette items at the beginning of the chapter, travelers need to know a few things about sleeping in shelters.

Most shelters will have a broom. Use it. Mice infest shelters because there is food. Less food on shelter floors means fewer mice scurrying about at night. Food should be consumed away from the shelter, though this is not always possible.

Because there are mice in some shelters, it is a good idea not to choose a sleeping spot along a wall and to point your head toward the opening of the shelter, as opposed to along the back wall. Mice use walls as cover, so you will notice less activity if you are situated away from the wall.

Most shelters will have "mouse hangers" (ropes hanging from the ceiling, usually with a plastic bottle threaded through the rope and a stick on the end). These are used to hang your backpack so mice do not gnaw through it to get to a crumb. When hanging your backpack in the shelter, unzip the pockets on your hip-belt or anywhere you may have left a morsel. The mice are going to get in one way or another; you might as well make it easy for them and save your pack from having a hole gnawed in it.

Also, these mouse hangers in shelters are not intended to take the place of hanging a bear bag. A shelter, like a tent, is not the place to store your food. Hang a bear bag on the provided pole or cable or place it in the bear box. If one of these options is not provided, hang your bag in a tree.

Every shelter will have a shelter log. These diaries are useful for learning about the highlights or dangers of the area or to write and read notes to and about other hikers. The logs are an indispensable source of information.

At one shelter everyone put their bear bags in the bear box provided by the trail club maintaining the shelter. In the morning every single bear bag had been chewed by rodents. After retrieving our bags I decided to peruse the shelter log while waiting for Chica to get ready, and there, along with some clever illustrations, was page after page of previous warnings about rodents in the bear box.

43. HOSTEL TIPS

The advantage of a hostel is that a single traveler

will spend less than at a hotel. Hostels are also part of the experience of a thru-hike and are typically filled with other hikers discussing the trail, playing music, and relaxing. Another benefit to hostels is they are typically located convenient to either the trail or town and will provide transportation to the trailhead or town as needed for free and most of them have laundry facilities.

The disadvantages of a hostel are the small, cramped rooms filled with multiple bunk beds and the uncomfortable bathroom-to-hiker ratio. It's a good idea to have earplugs for the snoring; they are beneficial in shelters and crowded tent sites as well.

There are two different types of hostels, paid and donation. The for-profit hostels charge a fee for the bunk, typically between $20 and $30 dollars. Other services like laundry or breakfast might be included or charged *a la carte*.

Hostels that operate on a donation basis are run by church organizations or "trail angels" (someone who provides unexpected help, food or shelter to a hiker at no cost). Please do not take donation to mean free. A donation should be equal to the cost of the bed at a for-profit hostel. If you are unable to pay, consider offering to help around the hostel. Hostels are time-consuming ventures and there is always something that needs to be done.

Most hostels have snacks and sodas available. These are typically purchased on an honor basis and are paid for when the tab is settled, usually the following morning. Hostel owners often also operate shuttles to neighboring towns or for slack-packing. Shuttles can be expensive and typical shuttle rates are between $1 - $2 a mile.

Hostels will usually have "town-clothes" for use in town while your filthy clothes are being laundered. These can be ill fitting, out of fashion, and hilarious. Perfect for "hiker trash" (a term lovingly applied to a thru-hiker).

Each hostel will have its own rules, which normally include the hostel's time for hiker midnight/lights out, a curfew for when the door will be locked, whether the bill can be paid with a credit card or cash only, and if the hostel allows work for stay.

44. TRAIL TOWN TIPS

Trail towns are a welcome break from constant hiking. They are a necessity for resupplying and showering off backpacker grunge. The trail bisects a few towns along the 2,200-mile route, but getting to most towns along the way will require a shuttle, hitch-hiking, or a long road-walk, as they will be one to ten miles from the trail.

Towns along the trail are accustomed to having thru-hikers and many often cater to the backpacking crowd. Many restaurants will have a "hiker burger" or other huge meal designed to refill the missing calories in a hiker's diet. Some grocery stores take care to stock hiking staples such as ramen noodles, tuna packets, tortillas, Knorr pasta/rice sides, instant mashed potatoes, Cliff bars, and trail mix.

Some towns, like Hanover, New Hampshire, go all out for the hikers. Hanover's restaurants lure hikers in with free offers like a complimentary slice of pizza at the Italian eatery or a free pastry at the local diner. Being the hometown of Dartmouth College, Hanover is an expensive town and affordable accommodations for hikers are not to be found. To encourage hikers to stay in town, residents open their homes for a night and host hikers. The organization, Hanover Area Friends of the AT, publishes a list of hiker resources and makes it available at the post office, library, and the Dartmouth Outing Club. We contacted a host the day before we arrived in town and were lucky enough to get a room on the first try and had a wonderful stay.

When in any trail town, even those that love thru-hikers, it's important to follow directions given to hikers. Many businesses do not want backpacks and poles taken inside, and you will often see a sign indicating this and a slew of packs lined up outside. Also, if at all possible, it is best to take a shower before going to grab grub. You might not be able to smell you, but non-hikers sure will.

V. BODY OF WORK
~ *Chica*

Taking care of your body is probably the most important thing you can do while on your multi-month wilderness trek. Your body is the vessel that will carry you over the 2,000 plus miles you need to achieve your AT thru-hiker status. We'll start with your feet, the most essential part of the hiker-body and then move on to the rest of your body.

FEET – THE ACHILLES HEEL OF THRU-HIKING

You know what's crazy? I hiked 2,189.8 miles without ever getting a blister, not even one. You know what's even more crazy? Neither did Sunsets.

We didn't know when we started that we would end up *never* getting a blister on our thru-hike; in fact, we fully expected to have blisters, or at least to get one or two over our six-months on the trail. And it was unusual to come across a hiker who did not have foot problems.

So, *how* did we traverse the whole trail without getting any blisters? We did research beforehand because we knew if we didn't take care of our feet, our thru-hike might end soon after it began. Here are our tips for you.

45. RESEARCH

Find out what others do to take care of their feet. Long distance running actually has a lot in common with long distance hiking, especially when it comes to your feet. A book we found helpful and thorough was *Fixing Your Feet - Injury Prevention and Treatments for Athletes* by John Vonhof. It is not a short book and is a bit dry, but it packs a punch with information and treatment remedies.

46. SOCKS

I wore a thin sock liner by Injinji, followed by a pair of Darn Tough merino wool light-cushion hiking socks.

Merino wool has several advantages. A four-season material, merino wool is not your grandmother's wool – it doesn't itch and it keeps you cool in hot weather and warm in cold weather. Hikers who do their laundry often, typically with no dryer sheets or fabric softener, will be happy to know this wool is static-free. It breathes and manages moisture extremely well – it can retain 30% of its own weight in moisture and still feel dry to the touch. It also dries quickly, which is a necessity for thru-hikers. Perhaps best of all, merino wool socks are odor resistant. Because of the effective moisture-wicking properties, odor-causing bacteria don't have the environment they need to thrive.

I had two pairs of both socks (two liners, two merino wool) and switched them out each day. If one pair was still wet the next morning (from water or sweat), I'd safety-pin them to my pack to dry in the sun while hiking. The Injinjis lasted my whole thru-hike. The Darn Toughs (which have a life-time warranty) started to wear. They didn't actually get holes in them, but I showed them to an outfitter who was a dealer for Darn Tough in Boiling Springs, PA and she said I needed a new pair. She gave me a very simple form to fill out and took care of sending my worn socks to Darn Tough while I picked out a new, similar pair at no cost. So easy. I can't say enough good things about Darn Tough – including the fact that my mom now wears them, and though she doesn't walk 20 miles a day, she is busy and walks around quite a bit everyday. They are the only socks she wears now!

The reason for wearing two socks each day? Because the Injinji socks fit around the toes like a glove, they prevent your toes from rubbing against each other which causes blisters. They also act as a "second skin" to create a barrier between your feet and the Darn Toughs. If you were to wear only one pair of socks, they might rub against the skin of your feet, forming hot spots and blisters, but the liner sock prevents this rubbing.

Note: Sunsets did not wear sock liners; he only wore Darn Tough medium-cushion socks. Also there are other merino wool brands besides Darn Tough; Smartwool is probably the second choice for thru-hikers, but there are several other brands as well.

47. SHOES/BOOTS

Because your feet swell slightly during the day, try to get fitted for your hiking shoes/boots in the afternoon after you've been on your feet for a while. Once you start thru-hiking, they will possibly swell even more. Also wear the exact type of socks (or socks combination) in which you will be hiking. You want your toes to have some wiggle room, but not too much room. If the foot slides around too much in your shoe, you'll have friction, which will lead to blisters. If your shoe is too tight, you'll also have friction, and your toes may be curled and smashed against the tip of your shoe. You want the perfect fit.

Choose a shoe or boot that is comfortable for you and your feet. Sunsets and I both chose trail runners: the Salomon X-Mission 3 Trail Runners for me, and the La Sportiva Wildcats for Sunsets.

Some people prefer hiking boots, but these would have been too rigid and heavy and would have taken forever to dry out. Your shoes will get wet frequently on the AT. A note about waterproof shoes/boots: because of how long you'll be hiking in the woods, and how often you'll hike in the rain or through puddles, mud and streams, even waterproof shoes will eventually become wet inside. And once that happens, good luck getting them dry; water cannot escape because of the waterproofing of said shoes.

If you have hiking boots, learn how to lace them properly for your specific needs. The correct method of lacing depends on how your feet feel and what kind of problems your feet have (https://www.rei.com/learn/expert-advice/lacing-hiking-boots.html).

48. INSOLES

Many hikers swear that having specific insoles in their shoes/boots helps their feet. I started my hike using the insoles that came in my trail runners, but switched to the Superfeet low-profile insoles in Damascus, VA. I believe they helped my sore feet be less sore each day. Sunsets used the insoles that came in his Wildcats.

If you do want to try insoles, please be fitted by an expert at a hiking shoe store. You will find several different kinds of insoles based on the shape and arch of your foot, and if you choose the wrong one, you could cause more problems than you solve.

49. PACK WEIGHT

While we did not go ultralight with our pack weight, we did work diligently to keep our weight as low as possible. It makes sense that the more weight you carry, the harder it is to walk a bazillion miles every day, and also the harder it is on your feet.

My pack, fully loaded with four days of food and two liters of water weighed in at 27 pounds. Sunsets' weight was about 30 pounds. Even though we weren't considered ultralight, we were much lighter than many packs out there (the heaviest I heard of was 65!), and this contributed to happier feet. Notice I did not say happy feet, but happ*ier*.

50. TRAINING

We trained for the AT hike with trail runners and our fully weighted packs. We were in Costa Rica at the time, so we used bags of rice and beans (the local cuisine) to fill our packs with the appropriate weight. We also lived in an area where there were no flat trails, so constantly going up and down hills at an elevation of 4,700 feet was really good training for us. This helped us know for certain that the trail runners we had chosen would work for us.

If you have some extra body weight on you, training can also help with losing this, which in turn will lighten the load for your knees and feet.

51. BUILD MILES SLOWLY

An important factor in our not getting blisters was that we slowly built up our daily mileage, especially early on. So many hikers we met started doing 14–20 mile days right away. They flew past us with tons of energy. But guess what? On our first zero day, only one full week into our hike, we found a ton of these same hikers sitting outside our motel in Hiawassee, GA. They were lounging on chairs with their feet up, icing injured parts, lancing blisters and visiting the hospital across the street.

I was determined to have us start our thru-hike by building up our miles slowly, even though it's a bit hard to do. Think of the beginning of a race: everyone is so excited in the beginning with tons of energy and endorphins; some people start the race going too fast, and then before they know it, they run out of gas, or worse, get injured and have to stop.

This is what we did:

* Week 1: 8 miles a day, with a zero day at the end of this week.

* Week 2: 10 miles a day, with a zero day at the end of this week.

* Weeks 3 and 4: 12 miles a day, with a zero day at the end of this week.

* Week 5 and on: 14 *or more* miles a day, with a zero day once a week.

* (after we got up to 18-20 miles a day, we started taking more neros than zeros.)

We stayed at 12 miles a day for two weeks because we listened to our bodies – they were screaming to have a few more days at 12 miles before bumping up to 14.

Your body will adapt, but you need to give it time. I remember in our first week feeling *there's no way I can hike more than eight miles a day.* In fact, I said this to Sunsets regularly. But guess what? I did. I felt the same way each week we increased our miles – *no way I can hike more than 10 miles, no way I can hike more than 12* – but we kept hiking. When we reached 14, we stayed at 14 for two-three weeks, and I thought we'd never be able to hike more than that a day. But we DID. Our bodies and feet became accustomed to what we were putting them through, and before we knew it, we were doing 20-mile days.

52. HOT SPOTS

A hot spot is an area of skin that feels hot, like when you get a rug burn or you rub something repeatedly on your skin and it gets red and slightly sore. As soon as you feel a hot spot, STOP immediately. A hot spot is your warning that a blister is about to form, but is not there quite yet. There's still time! Take off your shoes and tape the area with Leukotape or moleskin or whatever you prefer to use. The tape acts as a barrier between your skin and sock to stop the friction. The key is to stop as soon as you feel the first inkling of a hot spot and to have a plan for taping.

53. LUNCH BREAK

At lunchtime we always tried to take our shoes and socks off to let our feet air out and breathe. This probably doesn't sound like much of a tip, but our feet always felt so much better! Your socks become sweaty while you hike because every step of the Appalachian Trail is hard and you will be working. Taking your socks off helps dry your socks, as well as your feet and shoes. Let's face it – all three of them could use a good airing after several sweaty miles. Some people put clean/dry socks on at this point and hang the sweaty socks from their packs to dry.

54. SOAK

Those streams/springs where you get your water? They are also good for soaking your feet. Just make sure you go down stream from where people gather water.

The cold will help rejuvenate your feet and refresh you as well. Sometimes the water is so cold that it temporarily numbs your feet, which isn't bad either, especially if you are having foot pain. Think of it as icing an injury.

When in town you can soak as well; many hikers use Epsom salts to help with healing.

55. CAMP

As soon as we got to camp, we'd take off our shoes and socks and put on our camp shoes. Many hikers wear Crocs for their camp shoes, but I had Xero Z-Trails and Sunsets used dollar-store flip flops – both of these were extremely light. The Xero Z-Trails worked well for me, both in town and when I had rivers to ford in Maine; they strapped onto my feet and stayed there and helped balance me on the slippery rocks. Putting on your camp shoes right away lets your feet breathe and dry out, but also it feels so relaxing to take off your hiking shoes and to stretch out your toes.

56. STRETCHING

Most mornings I would stretch my feet, calves, and legs while eating my Pop-Tarts or protein bar. Associating breakfast with stretching helped me remember to stretch almost every day.

Also at night when lying in "bed," try moving your ankles in circles in the air.

Another stretch I liked to do while lying down was to hold my knee to my chest, alternating legs. This stretch hurts and feels so good at the same time that it will make you groan before you can stop yourself.

57. NAILS

Keep your toenails clipped short. Clip straight across the top, not a rounded cut. If you have long toenails, even if your shoes fit properly, your nails will stick out and press into the tip of your shoe, causing you pain, blisters, and possible bleeding. This can be even more noticeable when you are hiking down a steep slope. Some hikers' nails even turn black and fall off. I filed my nails after I cut them to smooth them out, so they wouldn't snag on socks or cause friction.

58. POWDER/CREAM

Frequently people use foot powder or petroleum jelly. We did not use either of these while hiking, but when we had a zero day at a hotel, we applied petroleum jelly to our feet and lay still on the bed to let it soak in. This softened the callouses that were forming.

THE REST OF YOUR BODY

Now let's talk about taking care of the rest of your body. You need not just your feet but your whole body to be functioning at its best to hike the whole Appalachian Trail.

59. TREKKING POLES

We felt that using trekking poles was like adding two extra limbs to our bodies. We used them going downhill when the steps down were huge, so we could put one pole down and lean our weight on it instead of jumping and losing our balance. We used them going uphill, and they almost acted like two extra arms that helped pull us up. I relied on my trekking poles so much that I developed my biceps without even trying! Some hikers do not use trekking poles, but the majority did use them and felt they were well worth the expense.

Side note: I also had problems with sore hands and I know this was from clenching my trekking poles harder than usual. When I'd wake in the morning, both of my hands, but particularly my left one, felt almost like what I think arthritis would feel like. To stretch them I would clench my hands tight into a fist, and then spread out my hands and fingers. Also try bending your fingers backwards, then forwards.

60. KT TAPE

KT Tape was very helpful to me for a variety of aches and pains. Honestly, I felt like some body part was bothering me almost every single day, the primary areas being my knees, shins, Achilles heels, ankles and feet. KT Tape works wonders and you can look up on YouTube how to wrap yourself for almost any injury or type of pain. The tape is very stretchy, and you use it to wrap the problem area (usually stretched tight on the problem area, and then looser towards the ends of the tape). It gives you more support when you hike and helps the problem area heal.

61. WET WIPE BATHS

At night after getting to camp and setting up our tent, we would both take a "wet wipe bath." Using one or two wet wipes (depending on how dirty we were), we would wipe down all the dirty and sweaty areas –

face, arm pits, stomach, legs, feet. This served two functions – to clean up a bit and to make us feel better before changing into our clean night clothes. So refreshing. Yes, you have to pack out the dirty wet wipes, but it was worth it for us.

HINT: Buy packages of 10-15 wet wipes or baby wipes at a time – the unscented ones are better for sensitive areas. Some hikers I knew bought baby wipes ahead of time and dried them out (hung on a line), then packed them in a bag; when needed, they simply added water to them. REI also sells a wipe that is dried into a tablet that looks like an Alka-Seltzer; just add water to make into a wet wipe.

62. OVERHEATING IN THE SUMMER

This was a real problem for Sunsets. Here are some things you can try that helped us: dip your buff or t-shirt in a stream and wring it out and put it back on; go for a swim; drink more water; stop and break in the shade more often. We stopped once every hour in the heat of the summer. Also, wear a sunhat and sunscreen. Some people wear a long-sleeved shirt and long pants for sun protection (some brands have sunscreen built into them).

Another thing we did that mitigated the heat was that we both started using a "cool rag." This is a small towel that you can dip in cold or warm water, wring out briefly, and then "whip it around," which brings air into it and makes it cool down. Then you can put it over your head, around your neck, or wherever you are most heated, and keep hiking. It will only stay cool for a while, but you can keep whipping it to make it cooler for as long as it stays wet (about three-four hours).

63. HYPOTHERMIA

Hypothermia happens when your body loses heat faster than it can produce heat. This is a very dangerous threat to a thru-hiker in windy or wet, cool conditions. As soon as you begin having any symptoms of hypothermia, stop at a shelter or put up your tent, strip and change into dry clothes, put on all your warm layers including hat and gloves, and get inside your sleeping bag. If you have an emergency blanket, put it on. Make hot coffee, hot chocolate or soup; ingesting warm liquids will help warm your body from the inside out.

Symptoms of hypothermia include:

* Shivering (usually the first sign).
* Mumbling or slurred speech.
* Breathing slow and shallow.
* Weak pulse.
* Lack of coordination, clumsiness.
* Very low energy or drowsiness.

* Confusion.
* Loss of consciousness.

64. SUN AND MOSQUITO PROTECTION

Though the Appalachian Trail is mostly in the woods and under tree coverage from the sun, you will find areas in which you will be fully exposed to the sun. Sunscreen is a must, especially for those with fair skin.

Sunsets and I both had sun hats with wide, bendable brims that effectively protected our heads, necks, and faces from the sun. Sunsets' hat also had a mesh net, which he could pull down to protect his face and ears from mosquitoes. I had a separate bug head-net for this purpose ($2 at Walmart) which worked great, especially while wearing my sunhat underneath – the brim of the hat kept the net from touching my face.

We also used an insect spray (Deep Woods OFF!) which worked sufficiently against the mosquitoes. There are several other products you can use as well.

The black flies in Maine can be a real problem, but luckily, by the time we got there at the end of August, it had cooled off and they were completely gone.

VI. CREATURE FEATURE
~ *Sunsets*

One of the best parts of the trail is the variety of animals a thru-hiker might happen to come across. In this chapter we will look at some of the animals you might encounter, including some that people fear.

In all, Chica and I were disappointed by the lack of wildlife. We hiked for 10 hours a day and slept in the wilderness just about every night, but we didn't see as much wildlife as we thought we would. Animals, in general, want nothing to do with humans... unless, of course, they can get a handout. But don't feed the animals!

My guess is, because we hiked as a couple and were often chatting with each other, we saw fewer animals than the solo hiker, but that is merely a theory. Here are a few of the animals you may see on a hike along the AT.

65. LARGE MAMMALS

Black Bear – *Ursus americanus*, the American black bear, is the only type of bear found on the length of the Appalachian Trail. It is also one of the most feared and talked about animals on the trail. Omnivorous and living in the high traffic areas of national and state parks, they have become accustomed to easy pickings from humans. Not humans themselves, mind you, just the food they have lying around or within easy reach of the bear. Therefore, hikers are strongly encouraged to store their food properly with bear cables or on a bear pole, in bear boxes, or by hanging a bear bag. Bears that have become accustomed to interacting with humans lose their fear of them and often become a nuisance.

An interesting thing happens to many thru-hikers; they start the trail with a fear of the black bear and then further down the trail, they eventually *want* to see them. We saw a total of four bears. One pair we saw as soon as we entered Shenandoah National Park. The young bears saw us and immediately scurried deep into the woods. The second two, also juvenile, were noshing on blueberries when we summited the top of a small mountain in New Jersey. They were surprised by us and, disoriented, ran a few steps towards us before changing course and trotting out of sight.

In addition to Shenandoah National Park and New Jersey, the Great Smoky Mountains National Park is known for black bear sightings. In black bear country, it is a good practice to whistle, talk or sing to let bears know you are in the area.

If you encounter a black bear, don't run and don't make eye contact. Never drop food to distract or appease the bear. If the bear has not seen you, you should slowly retreat from the bear. If it has seen you, make yourself known by talking calmly and assertively to the bear; the subject matter is inconsequential. Most likely it will move on about its business. If it seems interested in you, make yourself appear as large as possible.

Raise your arms with trekking poles over your head and make loud noises or yell. Black bears may stand on their hind legs, swat their paws at the ground, or even make a bluff charge whereby they run towards you but stop short of a maul. These are all opportunities for you to calmly (yeah, right) back away from the situation. Always make sure the bear has a way out as well – don't block its only path.

If the encounter escalates into an attack, which is rare, you need to fight and fight dirty. If you have bear spray, use it. Use your trekking poles. Pummel its snout with your fists and gouge its eyes with your fingers. Unlike with grizzly bears, playing dead does not work. You must fight. Oh, and black bears are faster than you could ever be, at both running and climbing trees. Sorry.

Moose – Populations of moose along the

Appalachian Trail start in Vermont for the NOBO hiker, although small populations exist as early as Massachusetts. They grow in numbers the further north you go with Maine having the largest population. The moose is the largest member of the deer family and can weigh up to 1,400 pounds.

Moose can be unpredictable and aggressive. It's important if you come across one to give it time to move along. Even though moose are more aggressive when they have a calf with them (spring) or during rutting season (fall), they can be so at anytime. If a moose becomes aggressive, put yourself in a position so that there is a sturdy tree or other structure between you and the moose. If this is not possible... *run*! Unlike with black bear aggression, with a moose you *should* run and if you get knocked down, curl up in a ball until the moose leaves.

Like all the other animals on the list, it is unlikely you will be attacked by a moose. It's probable that you won't even see one. But with all animals, give them space, don't molest them, and for the love of Pete, do not try taking that viral close-up selfie of you and a moose.

You will see a ton of evidence that moose are present in the form of huge moose-poop pellets along the trail, but not the moose themselves. If you want a chance to see a moose, they are most active early in the morning and in early evening and can often be seen at these times wading in ponds and eating the plant life from the lake bottom.

Leave No Trace Ambassador – Sightings of the LNTA, Bigfoot, Sasquatch, or whatever you call him have been made up and down the Appalachian Mountain corridor. Then again, a large amount of moonshine is produced along the Appalachian Trail as well.

Other Mammals – Deer are common along the trail and are often not easily spooked. You may also see rabbits, porcupines and raccoons.

You most likely will not see any of the large cats that exist along parts of the trail, such as cougars or lynx, as they are mostly nocturnal and secretive. And, though you won't see them, it is likely you will hear the canine cry of coyotes in the evenings.

66. RODENTS

You will see squirrels: red, grey, and tree, among others. The trail is even host to the flying squirrel, though you are unlikely to see one as they are nocturnal.

The rodents most hikers are concerned with, though, are those that share shelter space with the hikers. These are typically mice and chipmunks. These rodents, particularly the mice, can cause a fitful night of sleep as they scurry to and fro, sometimes across a shelter occupant's face. Although they are always drawn to easy meals left by sloppy hikers, the rodents also love backpacking gear and will often gnaw on dry bags, sleeping bags, and backpacks to acquire nesting material. Always use the provided mouse hanger in shelters. If there is not one, make one. Simply use another one as a template. Also, it's wise to unzip all of your pockets, particularly hip belt pockets. If a mouse does get to your bag, you want to give it easy access rather than having it burrow a hole in your gear.

It's not only those in shelters that need to be wary. We woke one morning to find our ShamWow cloths, which were attached to the outside of our packs, gnawed to strips by industrious rodents. Good thing when we bought them we followed the enticement to "Order Now" and received not one, but two sets.

We were tenting, well away from any shelter, and our packs were stored in the vestibule. After that night, we slept with the packs in our tent, which gave us the added benefit of being able to sleep with our feet elevated.

67. SNAKES ALIVE

Venomous snakes – "Uh, honey? Stop, turn around, and look at what you just stepped over."

These were the first words spoken directly after seeing my first timber rattlesnake along the Appalachian Trail. We were in Virginia and Chica had just stepped over the 14-inch venomous reptile, thinking it was a stick. To its credit, the snake simply lay there in the middle of the trail, seemingly unbothered by footfalls all around.

That wasn't our only close encounter with a rattlesnake. In our 2,200 miles of hiking, we saw a whopping 12 timber rattlesnakes. A couple of times they made their presence known with a distinctive shake, but just as often they lay stealthily silent, sometimes in the middle of the trail, sometimes in the tall grass paralleling the trail.

In addition to timber rattlesnakes, two other venomous snakes can be encountered on the trail. The first, the cottonmouth or water moccasin, is infrequently seen on the trail as its territory ends right about where the southern terminus begins in Georgia. Even though the snake could be found in the first 20 or so miles of the trail, this is unlikely as the trail climbs up and over mountains and the cottonmouth prefers lower elevations and water.

The third venomous snake found along the AT is the copperhead. They are most likely to be encountered along the AT from Georgia to New York. We did not see any copperheads or cottonmouths on our thru.

Although a bite from a venomous snake is unlikely, you should know what to do and, just as important, what not to do. The reality is, if you are bitten, you need antivenin. The faster you can get medical attention, the better off you will be. On the Appalachian Trail this may mean several miles and hours before you reach help.

First, let's talk about what not to do. Evidence suggests snakebite kits are ineffective and could even make the situation more dangerous. Do not buy or bring one. Forget everything you have seen in movies when someone is bitten. Do not cut an "X" around the bite with your knife. Do not try to suck the venom, and don't apply a tourniquet.

Great, so what should you do? The first step is to stay calm. Ha, I know! But really, try to calm down and walk a good distance from the snake and sit down. Remove any tight-fitting jewelry or clothing from the bite area, as it is going to swell. Call 911 if you have a cell signal. Use a pen or sharpie to mark the edge of swollen areas every 15 minutes; this can help medical personnel determine the extent of envenomation. And finally, hike out to the nearest road, with another hiker if available, and get to a hospital as quick as possible.

According to Wikipedia, "It has been estimated that 7,000-8,000 people per year receive venomous bites in the United States, and about five of those people die." So, it is unlikely you will be bitten in the first place, and highly unlikely you will die from the bite. You can further your chances of remaining unbitten by being cognizant of where you are placing your hands when rock scrambling or gathering wood – both places where a snake might be hanging out. It's sad that it needs to be said, but don't handle snakes, don't get close to try and get that epic selfie, and if you see one or hear one, give it a wide berth.

All in all, we saw a total of 37 snakes over our six months on the trail, 12 venomous and the rest nonvenomous.

Nonvenomous – Of the nonvenomous snakes we saw, garter snakes, milk snakes and black rat snakes make up the majority. We saw multiple examples of each with the black rat snakes being the most impressive. They can reach up to seven feet in length and are intimidating but also are timid and avoid confrontation. They will shake their tail against dead leaf material to simulate a rattlesnake.

Another snake deserving of an Academy Award, due to its dramatic defense mechanisms, is the eastern hognose snake. We had a general rule that if a snake was in the middle of the trail, we would leave it, if we could get around it. Rattlesnakes we would move off the trail, even if we could get around them, because it would create an emergency if someone stepped on one. But normally we just walked around snakes.

When we came upon the hognose I wasn't sure what it was. I was sure that we couldn't easily go around it. I did identify it as nonvenomous, so keeping a reasonable distance away, I touched the tip of my trekking pole to the snake's tail. That's when the performance began. The hognose curled into an S shape and simultaneously let out a loud "hssssssss," puffed up its neck like a pissed-off cobra and inflated its body. After so much bluster, the snake finally slithered off. However, had I pushed it a bit farther, the snake would have pretended to strike or even flip over on its back, stick out its tongue and play dead. Despite the theatrics, the snake is harmless and docile. It's unusual to see one on the trail and we (well, maybe not Chica) considered ourselves fortunate.

68. AMPHIBIANS

The eastern newt is one of the most frequent amphibians you will come across, more specifically, the red eft stage of the newt's life. This is when the newt develops lungs and leaves the water, at least for a while. The newt turns a bright orange that warns of its toxicity and stands out from the brown forest floor.

We saw hundreds of these little guys, always right in the middle of the trail. Cute little buggers.

In addition to the eastern newt, you will most likely encounter other salamanders. By the way, all newts are salamanders, but not all salamanders are newts. Salamanders are terrestrial while newts are both aquatic and terrestrial. In addition to the salamanders, you will encounter many different types of frogs and toads along the trail. Sometimes you will only hear them as they croak and peep around ponds and streams.

69. TICKED OFF

It was raining… again. We were tired of being wet, so we called the closest hostel, The Rock and Sole, to reserve a room. They had a private trailer, nicknamed Trashy, which was perfect for us. Once we arrived at the hostel, we saw that one of our friends was there too. He had been feeling under the weather with fatigue and was taking some time off.

Later that afternoon he found a tick on his shoulder and had the hostel owner help him remove it. Shortly afterwards I heard him exclaim, "Shit." He walked over and asked, "Does this look like a bulls-eye rash to you?" Well, if that wasn't a bulls-eye mark, I don't know what would be. This circle-shaped rash is present in 70-80% of Lyme disease cases.

Our buddy went to a local clinic where a Lyme disease test was performed. It was positive and a round of antibiotics were prescribed. We connected with him several weeks later and his symptoms had vanished and all was well.

Ticks may be small creatures, but they get a tip all their own. Of all the animals mentioned above, ticks are the thru-hiker's biggest nemesis. While Lyme disease, transmitted by the deer tick (aka black-legged tick), is the most common, ticks can transmit other ailments including Rocky Mountain spotted fever, carried by the wood tick, and the lone star tick transmits the causative agent of southern tick-associated rash illness. Each tick variety can cause multiple illnesses. Ticks are located all along the trail and often get picked up by the hiker in tall grass.

Ticks that have been attached for less than 24 hours

are unlikely to have infected you with Lyme or any other disease. Daily tick checks can help spot climbers and those that may have attached. One of the problems, though, is that the main culprit of Lyme disease, the deer tick, is often in nymph form and tiny – the size of a poppy seed – and difficult to spot. Light colored clothing can help you see the climbers.

Also, treating your clothes and gear with permethrin will help kill ticks. Permethrin can be bought and applied by the hiker; some clothing companies have permeated their products with the chemical; or you can send your clothes to be treated to InsectShield.com. The last two are preferable, as the treatment will last for a full thru-hike (70 washings) as opposed to only seven washings for self-treated spray. Besides ticks, permethrin also helps prevent against mosquitos, flies, ants, chiggers, midges and fleas.

VII. PEEING, POOPING, PERIODS & PRIVIES
~ *Chica*

Our bodies have certain functions, and most of us are used to doing our bathroom duties in an actual bathroom – a flushing toilet, soap, warm water, *etc*. At most shelters there are privies, but we guarantee there won't always be one when you need it. You're going to have to go in the woods at some point. And by "go," I mean pee, poop and, if you're a female, take care of your period.

70. PEEING (FOR WOMEN)

This is for the girls only because, guys, you know what to do.

There are several devices on the market that will enable you to pee standing up like a guy, and I knew many women hikers who used these and loved them. Some examples of brands are: Pstyle, GoGirl, Venus to Mars, and Peebuddy. I did not experiment with or use any of these.

I just went *au naturel* in the woods. I would first find either a log or tree trunk to use for support. No matter how fit your thigh and calf muscles are, when hiking all day every day, you will need support to lean on. While some hikers use a small tree in front of them to grasp, others use a vertical log behind them for support – find out what your own preferences are (I varied between both). Then I would pull my shorts and underwear down to my ankles, squat, use one hand to pull my clothes away from my shoes as I didn't want to pee on my clothes, and the other to support myself, and then I let it flow. I had my "pee rag" handy, used it quickly once to pat dry, then pulled up my shorts and was done.

A pee rag is a bandana that you use to dry yourself after peeing. You can tie it onto the back of your backpack, and the sun will bleach and dry it out during the day so there is no scent. Really, this works. When you get to town, throw it in the wash with your regular laundry.

I became so comfortable with peeing in the woods, I sometimes would do it even if there was a privy available. Because there was sometimes a line at the privies, it was quicker to run into the woods behind our tent and much more private. Besides, the privies stink.

71. POOPING

Pooping in the woods calls for the same scenario as above, but you will need to have your "TP bag" with you (toilet paper bag should include a trowel, toilet paper, wet wipes if you use them, and hand sanitizer). Follow the steps below for a successful session in the woods.

First, don't go until you're ready. You don't want to be squatting forever, your leg muscles will not allow for this. This is not the time to pull out a magazine and relax. You have doo to do.

Second, select a spot at least 70 paces (about 200 feet) from the trail, water sources or campsites. A support log or tree trunk is helpful. Sometimes when I was in a hurry, I just squatted with my two hands behind me on the ground for support.

Third, use your trowel or stake to dig a hole 6" deep.

Fourth, squat and do your business in the hole.

Fifth, use as little toilet paper and/or wet wipes as possible. Toilet paper goes in the hole; wet wipes (even the biodegradable ones) must be packed out.

Sixth, bury your shit (couldn't resist) and cover up the hole with dirt.

Seventh (man, there are so many steps!), push a stick into the ground, close to the hole, so other hikers will know not to dig there.

Eighth, use your hand sanitizer.

HINT: When you find your secluded spot to go pee

or poop, make sure the trail does not wrap around by your spot. This happened to me a couple of times – I guess I was always more "hurry up and go" while Sunsets took his time to go deep into the woods and find a "for sure" secluded spot. The trail winds and zigzags sometimes, so just be aware of this. The last thing you want when you're squatting with your bare bum exposed to the world is to be surprised by a fellow hiker coming upon you doing your business.

72. PERIODS (GALS ONLY)

We have a variety of choices for dealing with our period on a multi-month thru-hike. Several birth control options allow you to skip your period for several months; ask your doctor.

A period cup, such as the DivaCup, makes having a period pretty easy. No tampons needed, and you just empty the cup every 12 hours. Research the options, then try them and be comfortable with them *before* you start the AT.

As for me, I went the old-fashioned route and used o.b. tampons, which do not have a separate plastic applicator (you use your finger to guide the tampon in), but only a very thin, plastic outer wrapper. I felt these would make the least amount of trash for me to carry out. You must not bury your tampons on the trail, nor can you leave them in the privies. I had a separate, heavy-duty ziplock bag that I put duct tape over so you couldn't see inside it and deposited my used tampons in this. Yes, this sounds gross, but you absolutely have to carry them out. I kept this ziplock bag in my TP kit and would hang with my food bag each night. You can also put a dry tea bag in the ziplock bag to help absorb the odor.

73. PRIVIES

A privy on the AT is defined as a small box, sometimes enclosed by a structure, sometimes not (as we experienced), placed over a hole in the ground where human waste is to be deposited. Privies are mainly located at the shelters along the trail, although some shelters do not have privies, and sometimes (rarely) we would come across a privy on the trail with no shelter.

We can't tell you how many times we've been asked how we prevent germs when using the privies. It's actually pretty hard to do, and the truth is, we didn't even try. You don't have enough excess toilet paper to place around the lid (if there *is* a lid; sometimes it's just a hole cut into a wood plank). Our best advice is to look before sitting (to make sure no excrement is on the lid), and then sit yourself down, use it, and then clean yourself with toilet paper, wet wipes and hand sanitizer.

Keep in mind that ONLY human waste and toilet paper can go into the privy hole – no tampons, wet wipes (even if biodegradable), or wrappers of any kind.

If you don't like the privies, it can be quite peaceful and even more sanitary to simply go in the woods.

VIII. SPECIFIC SPECIFICATIONS
~Sunsets

Freedom is part of the allure of thru-hiking the Appalachian Trail. Far from the constraints of an 8-5 job, long-distance hikers become accustomed to and embrace the ability to wake when they desire, to walk the distance they choose, and while abiding by Leave No Trace principles, to set up camp and to sleep where they want.

For the most part, there are few rules on the AT, but those that exist are sometimes difficult to unravel, as if a bureaucratic committee compiled them. Below we'll address the four areas that seem to cause the most confusion, stress, and frustration for the thru-hiker, and we'll also provide some specific tips for the most photographed location along the trail, McAfee Knob.

74. HOLY SMOKES

It's no wonder Great Smoky Mountains National Park (GSMNP or the Smokies) has rules. Logging 11.3 million visitors in 2016, GSMNP is the most visited national park out of 59 in the U.S. Guess how many of those visitors are thru-hikers? Not many. Thru-hikers are like a couple of grains of sand on a beach. So, when it seems like the rules are encouraging you, the thru-hiker, not to linger in the park, you are right. And what are these rules I keep talking about?

First up, you will need a printed permit per hiker. You can obtain these at their website: https://smokiespermits.nps.gov. To qualify for the AT thru-hiker permit, your hike must start and end at least 50 miles outside the GSMNP. In addition, the thru-hiker can only travel on the Appalachian Trail while in the park. If you do not meet these requirements, you should apply for the general backcountry permit, also available on the website.

You must have your permit on your person while in the park. We ran into two "ridge runners" (people who educate hikers, enforce regulations, perform trail and shelter maintenance) while hiking in the park. One asked to see the permit, the other didn't. You can be fined for not having one, so print it and put it in a ziplock bag. There is a reason they're called "smoky" mountains – they are constantly covered in clouds, which means your stuff is going to get wet.

You can print the permit up to 30 days before you expect to be in the park. We printed ours right before we left home, and even with our moderately slow pace, had several days to spare (we entered the park on day 24 of our hike). If you do not print them at home, there are hostels and motels on both north and south ends of the park where you can access the internet and print the permit.

One last thing about the permit before covering the other rules – once you enter, you are only allowed eight days in the park. The length of the AT through GSMNP is roughly 72 miles; therefore, you must hike an average of nine miles per day to finish in eight. Keep in mind, Gatlinburg, TN is accessible about halfway through the Smokies and most thru-hikers can't resist a visit to the tourist destination. Keep this in mind as you plan your mileage around the eight-day time constraint.

The next rule was the one that caused me the most handwringing. By the time we hit GSMNP, I had decided that sleeping in shelters would never be my preference. Even better, we were getting in the habit of utilizing campsites that were not associated with shelters. We found we enjoyed the solitude of tenting alone.

This is not possible as you travel through the Smokies. Hikers are required to sleep in shelters. Actually, the rule is a catch-22. Thru-hikers cannot make reservations for the shelters but are required to sleep in them, unless they are full. However, thru-hikers must give up their space in the shelter if someone comes in with a reservation (non-thru-hikers must make reservations). Joseph Heller would be proud.

Because I had such an aversion to sleeping in shelters, and it seemed we were destined to do so, we developed a strategy. We would sleep in each morning and plan each day so that we would enter a shelter area as late in the day as possible. We were in a "bubble" (a large group of hikers hiking the same mileage each day) and it was probable, if we did this, the shelters would be full… and they were. We tented (legally!) every day we spent in the Smokies.

And you might think that the whole reservation thing is never a problem, but it was on our last day. We arrived at the shelter to chaos. The shelter was full, save three spots reserved, and all the tent spots were taken. The ridge runner opened an expanded tent site to accommodate the mass. Just around dark, the ridge runner came through the overflow camp letting us know to tell any new arrivals that they were not to tent but had to occupy the three spaces in the shelter. Apparently the reservers didn't show.

One last bit of information about hiking through GSMNP – you won't find many privies.

For most of the Appalachian Trail, one finds a privy

at almost every shelter, even a few along the way that are nowhere near a shelter. At one point in our journey through the park, there was a "toilet area" off a side trail not far from camp. I called this "Shit Hill" as visible feces and toilet paper were strewn from hundreds of hikers who had all pooped in a relatively small area. It was gross, and I still do not understand how that is better than erecting a privy. Now you know.

75. SHENANDOAHS

Shenandoah National Park (SNP or the Shennies) is a moderate to "easy" 100 miles of the Appalachian Trail located completely in the state of Virginia. Like the Smokies, the Shennies require a permit for backcountry camping. Unlike GSMNP, the permit for the SNP is free and you only need one for a party of up to 10 hikers. There is a kiosk at each end of the park with permits available.

SNP is a favorite of thru-hikers. Not only is the terrain pleasant, but those wishing to see a bear are likely to experience a sighting in this park. Two of the four bears Chica and I saw during our hike were in SNP. Long-distance hikers also love the camp stores and wayside restaurants throughout the park. Once again, like GSMNP, the park receives a tremendous number of visitors. Most are in cars and are in the park for only a day or two. Visitors will find ample sources of food and shopping, which might be why bears are more apt to make themselves known. For the hiker, this is great; it means a burger and a blackberry shake almost every day if one so desires… and you will desire. I am serious when I say you must budget for the Shennies.

Aside from the permit, the other main concern for thru-hikers are the camping rules. Like the GSMNP, campsites are restricted in the Shennies. The following guidelines for choosing a campsite are taken from the official website for SNP (https://www.nps.gov/shen/planyourvisit/campbc_regs.htm):

"Allow time in your trip to look for a legal, comfortable, and safe place to camp. It is strongly recommended that camping occur at pre-existing campsites. These campsites have been created and established by prior visitor use and are not posted, signed, or designated by the park. Use only campsites that are at least 20 yards from a park trail or unpaved fire road. Remember, good campsites are found, not made!

"Campsites must be:

* At least 10 yards away from a stream or other natural water source.

* At least 20 yards away from any park trail or unpaved fire road.

* At least 50 yards away from another camping party or no camping post sign.

* At least 50 yards away from any standing buildings and ruins including stone foundations, chimneys, and log walls. Our historic resources are valuable and fragile.

* At least 100 yards away from a hut, cabin, or day-use shelter.

* At least 1/4 mile away from any paved road, park boundary, or park facilities such as campgrounds, picnic grounds, visitor centers, lodges, waysides, or restaurants."

Finally, backcountry fires are not allowed in SNP – no s'mores for you.

76. HOB KNOBBING

McAfee Knob is arguably the most photographed spot on the Appalachian Trail. Even if you don't know it by its name, I am certain you have seen the photos of hikers precariously perched on the end of a huge rock jutting out seemingly hundreds of feet in the air.

Here's a secret – it's not as scary as it looks. Though

the optical illusion gives the impression that the ledge is a great height from the ground below, the reality is that it is only about a 30-foot drop. In addition, the part hikers sit on for that epic photo slants up slightly, so as you sit, you are leaning back and not forward toward the abyss. I could be wrong, but I searched and searched and was unable to find any story of a hiker falling off the rock.

Because it is so popular, other hikers will probably be there to take your picture. Also, because of the popularity, camping at the rock is prohibited. You will find an official campsite about a mile past the knob (NOBO) and many hikers hike back for the morning sunrise. The orientation makes McAfee perfect for sunrise shots. For sunsets, nearby Tinker Cliffs is your best bet.

77. THE WHITES

The White Mountains of New Hampshire are intimidating for many reasons. First is the shear massiveness of the mountains. The terrain is unlike any experienced up to that point (NOBO) on the AT. Also, the weather in this region is some of the most severe in the United States with Mt. Washington recording the second highest land wind speed on record, 231 mph. If you sent clothes home for the summer, you should have them mailed back by the time you hit the Whites.

The trails through this section predate the Appalachian Trail and they have multiple names, none of which include the word Appalachian in them. A guidebook or maps are a necessity here.

A hiker's pace slows down through the Whites and southern Maine. Plan to slow down between 25% and 50% of what you were hiking prior to the beginning of the Whites – it is that much of a change. If you were consistently doing 20-mile days, expect to only do 12-15 (sometimes less!).

Like other areas of high use along the trail, there are rules for camping in the Whites. Distilled down, the rules are simple: no camping above tree-line (alpine areas) and campsites need to be a quarter mile from lakes, other campsites, roads, and huts. For complete information view the .pdf from the U.S. Forest Service here:

https://www.fs.usda.gov/Internet/FSE_DOCUMENTS/stelprdb5363715.pdf.

The Appalachian Mountain Club (AMC) manages trails and huts in the Whites and southern Maine. A hut is a building with rooms for bunks, a kitchen, and a privy. The huts are often shunned by thru-hikers because the cost of staying in one is often prohibitive as they are designed for weekend warriors, not long-distance hikers. That said, the huts can be useful. All huts have water, affordable food, restrooms with real soap, and caretakers that are knowledgeable about the area.

Work for stay is also a strategy for the thru-hiker. In exchange for cleaning or doing dishes, hikers are given a place indoors for the night. Your bed will be the dining room floor, but for most thru-hikers that's preferable to paying $100 or more for a bunk. Work for stay is first come, first served and is given at the discretion of the crew. In other words, if you are an ass, don't expect to be able to do work for stay. When the weather is dangerous, huts will make room for as many thru-hikers as needed.

We stayed in one hut – Lake of the Clouds, which is a great hut to set you up to summit Mt. Washington. Because it comes up right before Mt. Washington (NOBO), Lake of the Clouds is usually crowded with many paying customers and can accommodate many hikers who want to do work for stay. Another option at this hut is THE DUNGEON. Being a small, dank cellar located around the back of the building with just enough room for six mattress-less bunks, the accommodations live up to their name. For the hiker who prefers to eschew work for stay (me), the dungeon is available for $10 a bunk.

You can get through the Whites without staying in huts. The AMC also runs campsites with tent platforms and shelters. The sites or shelter spaces cost $10 for the first stay and $5 thereafter. This special rate is for thru-hikers only and is implemented using a punch card that you receive at the first shelter or site at which you stay. The card also entitles you to one free bowl of soup and two free baked goods at any of the huts. We stayed at almost all these tent sites and they were great. Each one has a caretaker on site and all the tents sites had platforms, which we came to love.

We stopped at almost all of the huts, mainly for water fill-ups (no filtering needed!), bathroom breaks, and to wash our hands. We could sit down inside at the tables and take a break even if we didn't buy any of their food.

One final hint – if you pass by a hut mid-morning, stop in and ask if there are leftovers. Since the huts are remote, all goods must be hiked in and all refuse must be hiked out. When there are leftovers, it's a win/win. You get a free meal and less garbage needs to be packed out.

78. BAXTER STATE PARK (BSP)

For the NOBO thru-hiker, the culmination of almost 2,200 miles is a spectacular hike through the 100-

mile wilderness followed by a climactic summiting of Mt. Katahdin. Most thru-hikers lay up for their summit bid by sleeping overnight in Baxter State Park. From Baxter, Mt. Katahdin is a strenuous five-mile hike up and then you must come back down.

You have two options for camping the night before summit day. Katahdin Springs is a sprawl of lean-to shelters and tent sites. While many sites are available, Katahdin Springs campground is busy and you usually need to make reservations a week or more in advance. The problem with this, of course, is the thru-hiker can't always plan that far ahead of time. Injury, weather, or some other factor may cause a hiker to change their summit day. So, Katahdin Springs, while an option, is not optimal. One hiker we knew reserved a tent spot at Katahdin Springs for an entire week, and since each site can have multiple tents, allowed other thru-hikers he knew to stay at his spot.

The second and preferred option is staying at The Birches. This camp spot is solely for NOBO thru-hikers and costs $10 per person whether you stay in the shelter or tent. There are only 12 spots available at The Birches and hikers must sign up at the kiosk at the park entrance. When we hiked, we were worried about not getting a spot. We arrived at the kiosk around 3 p.m. on a Friday after enjoying an overpriced but incredible burger and beer at the camp store just before the park. Even though we were right in the middle of a thru-hiker bubble, only eight names were above ours and empty spots were still available in the camp that night. If the chart is full, you can stealth camp before entering the park, but there are no spots available once in Baxter.

You have two additional options. First, you could camp about 15 miles from the summit and hike the easy 10 miles to one of the aforementioned campsites, then keep going the additional 5 miles to summit the same day. Remember, you must also come back down, making the total hike about 20 miles; the five up Katahdin and down again are pretty difficult. After that long day, you would then need to stay at Katahdin Springs with a reservation or hitch into Millinocket, about 45 minutes away, to stay for the night.

The last option is to hitch or take a scheduled shuttle to Millinocket for the night. Shower and get a full belly before coming back the next morning to summit. The hostel in town, the AT Lodge (http://appalachiantraillodge.com), can help with shuttles. Cell service is non-existent in Baxter State Park, so you would be wise to contact the Lodge about shuttle service on the last mountaintop before reaching Abol Bridge. The camp store has a satellite phone they may let you use.

So, that takes care of options for scheduling your summit day. Baxter has a few more hoops for you to jump through to complete this epic journey. The next section is taken from Baxter State Park's website (https://baxterstatepark.org/general-info/the-at/) and concerns the new (as of 2016) thru-hiker registration system that is in place.

"All AT hikers (northbound, southbound, section and flip-flop) must secure an AT Hiker Permit at the Katahdin Stream campground ranger station before attempting to summit.

"Details about permit system for AT hikers:

1. AT hiker permit cards will be available when the Hunt Trail opens to hiking in the spring (usually in early June).

2. AT hiker permit cards must be secured in person at Katahdin Stream campground ranger station. Hikers must provide their actual name, trail name and an emergency contact phone number to receive a card.

3. There is no fee for a card.

4. The cards will be issued to four categories of long-distance AT hikers: northbound, southbound, section and flip-flop. Each hiker

will be required to self-determine and declare their category prior to being issued an AT hiker permit card.

5. The available number of AT hiker permit cards for 2017 will be 3,150.

6. Hikers must stop at the Katahdin Stream ranger station to obtain their permit and yellow hiker registration sheet. Please note that this does not exempt hikers from the need to sign trail registers.

7. Permit cards will be date-stamped at the time of issue. Permit cards are valid for a period of seven days from the date stamp on the card. For example, a permit card date stamped 9/23/17 will be valid through 9/30/17.

8. If all available 2017 permit cards have been issued, registration of AT hikers will end for the season, the long-distance hiking campsite will be closed and normal access protocols will apply to AT shuttle traffic arriving at Togue Pond gatehouse.

9. If all available cards have been issued, AT hikers may still complete their hike by entering the park through the Togue Pond gate following the same process as other day use or camping visitors."

Before starting the hike up the mountain, most thru-hikers leave their full packs at the ranger station. The station has daypacks you can use for water and snacks and all you need to bring is rain gear or a jacket in case you need it. If you think about it, you won't need any of your other gear, so why lug it up there? We didn't even take our trekking poles. I know, I know, there are purists who insist they take their pack up. If this is you, knock yourself out. For everyone else, you have the option to slack-pack Katahdin.

Whew! We are almost done. One last thing – getting down from Katahdin… of course there are options. The official trail up the mountain is the Hunt Trail, but once you summit, you are officially done (congratulations) and can come down a different way. After scrambling up some of the sections on Hunt, you may not want to go down that way again. The other two options are going down the Abol Trail or continuing on the Knife Edge.

After summiting, Chica and I descended the Abol Trail, which is a bit shorter than Hunt. Once we were at the tree line, the trail was pleasant, but before that, it was steep hiking on loose rock. At the end of Abol Trail, you will need to road-walk or hitch back to the ranger station at Katahdin Streams to get your pack and return the daypack (if necessary). Hitching within the park is easy. Getting a ride into Millinocket may be more challenging. To reiterate, there is no cell service in Baxter, so any shuttle service needs to be prearranged. Once again, check with the AT Lodge as they frequently have a sign-up sheet for a shuttle.

The Knife Edge starts at the summit of Katahdin and hiking it can vary between scrambling over boulders to practically rock-climbing. For some, it is the best way to finish their thru. Utilize Awol's *Guide* for options of getting to town from the Knife Edge.

Okay... Katah-DONE!

The reason we included this chapter is that these are the areas (except McAfee) that stressed us out. In spite of all the hiker chatter about speeding through the Smokies, struggling through the Whites, and jumping hoops at Baxter so that you can summit Katahdin, you may find it all much ado about nothing. These areas may have more rules than the rest of the AT, but once you are through them, you'll wonder what all the fuss is about.

IX. FUEL & MAINTENANCE
~ Chica

Our body is the vehicle we used to travel over 2,200 miles on the Appalachian Trail. We have already discussed keeping our vehicle mechanically sound by taking care of our feet and other body parts. In this chapter, we will talk about fueling our machine to keep the wheels turning (er, feet moving).

79. IN THE BEGINNING

Don't pack too much food in the beginning! We made this mistake as everyone kept telling us, "You'll need the calories!" However, our "hiker hunger" (when hikers have far more hunger than usual) did not kick in until about three weeks after we started. We had packed separate Knorr Rice Sides for our dinners each night, but the first couple of weeks we ended up sharing only one of them between us. Even Sunsets, who in everyday life could eat a whole one for his dinner, could not do so the first couple weeks on the trail.

Our hiker friends also experienced not being very hungry on the trail in the beginning. They would eat large quantities in trail towns – AYCE (all-you-can-eat) buffets were quite popular – but on the trail, they simply were not that hungry. In fact, they talked about forcing themselves to eat, as they knew they needed to for the energy.

Our advice for the first week or two of hiking is to pack high-energy foods, but keep in mind that you may not able to eat more calories than usual until further into your trek.

80. SICK OF STUFF

You know what happens when you eat a Knorr Rice Side every day for several weeks straight? The very thought of that ooey-gooey not-quite-done rice and sauce makes you want to gag.

Yep, we got sick of Knorr Rice Sides *very* quickly; Sunsets could not stomach them at all after the first week. We also went through several brands of protein bars before we found one that was appetizing to both of us (Nature Valley protein bar, which was more like a candy bar than a highly dense protein bar).

Keep in mind that your tastes can change, and you may develop an aversion to certain foods or crave other things that you've never before thought of eating.

81. EAT WHAT YOU WANT

We are not nutritionists or doctors, and to be honest,

we were not very health conscious on our thru-hike. We felt like we had so many other things to think about without spending time on exact proportions of protein, carbs and fats.

So, what did we do?

In all our lazy glory, we ate what we wanted to eat – both on the trail and in town. This might be the only time in your life, outside of being a teenager, that you can eat with impunity. Dig in! The only thing we looked for was calories, protein and sometimes salt content; the higher the numbers the better – the exact opposite of everyday life.

Once you get going and your body becomes used to the fact that you are hiking 10-20 miles a day, there will be no way to ingest as many calories as your body is burning. Also, you won't be able to carry the weight of the mass quantity of food your body actually needs. Not everyone loses weight on the trail, but most do. Sunsets and I sure did – he lost 55 pounds and I lost 38.

82. SHIPPING BOXES

Many hikers prepare boxes for their entire journey ahead of time and have someone at home ship them throughout their hike to various trail towns.

Some hikers spent a great deal of time prior to their hike freeze-drying their own foods. Our friend, Mystic, made her own freeze-dried packaged meals in ziplock bags and only had to add boiling water to make great meals that tasted amazing. Her husband sent her the boxes when she told him where she'd be and when. She claimed her food bag weighed much less because of the lightness of freeze-dried food.

Some reasons you might *not* want to ship boxes include: expensive postage, not knowing beforehand what you want or how much you will need, complicated logistics, and needing to have a point person at home. One day we hit three trail magics (it was a great day!) and didn't touch the food we were carrying. We consequently had extra food, and if we had been scheduled to receive a resupply box, we would have had even *more* excess food. On the other hand, if you are in charge of buying your own food each time you arrive in town, you can easily take into account what you still have and not overbuy.

At every town on the trail you can get food supplies, so if you don't want to ship boxes to yourself, you can easily get by without doing so. Each time you stop in a trail town, simply buy enough food to last until the next town.

83. PICKING UP YOUR PACKAGE

If you have boxes shipped to post offices along the way, keep in mind that the post offices are only open at certain hours. Refer to Awol's *Guide* for exact hours of each post office. All post offices are closed on Sundays, most are only open for limited hours on Saturdays, and some are even closed for a two-hour lunch during the week, which makes it difficult to retrieve your package. Depending on the weather, your health, or other disruptions of your plans, you will continuously change your mileage and schedule. We didn't think it was a big deal (*sure, we'll get there M-F before five, no problem*), but no matter how hard we planned, we ended up at the post office late or on the wrong day.

A better idea is to utilize hostels for your resupply packages, even if you don't end up staying there. They are always open so you can retrieve your package no matter what day or time you arrive in town. Even if you have to pay a buck or two if you're not staying there, it may be worth it.

84. EXPERIMENT

Don't be afraid to experiment with different foods on the trail. I craved hummus, Triscuits and kalamata olives, so I packed them out for lunch for a while. It gave me something to look forward to all morning long. Yes, it was a bit messy with the olives and hummus (I double-bagged them), but it was worth it to me – at least for a while.

Surprisingly, cheese became a staple for us. We bought the hard cheeses like sharp cheddar, colby and gouda; they kept better, even in the warmer weather. We also ate cold chicken nuggets (from grocery store deli) in tortilla wraps with mayonnaise or barbeque sauce – delicious! A tortilla filled with peanut butter, trail mix and dried fruit (think apples or bananas) is not bad either. Sunsets even carried a glass jar of pickles one week, because he craved salt so badly (not recommended, quite heavy!).

The food combinations we tried in no way compared to those of other hikers. Imagine these: a Spam and honey bun sandwich (or Spam with anything!), Doritos and cheese tortilla wraps, hot or cold ramen noodles with tuna and peanut butter, slices of white bread dipped into a can of cake frosting, or canned Vienna sausages on crackers. You get the picture.

85. CARE PACKAGE TIPS

If someone wants to send you a care package on the trail, I highly suggest you give them a list of what to pick and choose from. Better yet, give them an exact list. You do not want to get excess items that you cannot use or have to give away. Tell them exactly what you want and need so they can't go wrong. Then if you're still missing something, you can easily pick it up in town before getting back on the trail.

Here's a few examples of things we looked forward to receiving in care packages:

* Mountain House or Back Pantry freeze-dried meals (we didn't buy these for ourselves as they were expensive, but they made an excellent no-fuss treat!).

* Beef jerky (we LOVE beef jerky and it's an excellent source of protein).

* Trail mix and dried fruit.

* Candy (be specific – our favorites were Jolly Rancher hard candies, Sour Patch Kids, SweetTarts minis, peanut butter M&M's and candy bars of any kind).

* Ziplock bags (different sizes – used for everything from food storage to pain pills to keeping cells phones dry in the rain).

* One roll of toilet paper (we'd split it up between us; no need to carry the weight of a whole roll at any one time).

* Wet wipes and/or small hand sanitizer.

* Vitamin I (ibuprofen) or Aleve (naproxin). I don't even want to think about how much of this we used!

* Small bag of homemade cookies/bars to enjoy right away!

86. BEAR BAGGING TIPS

A bear bag or food bag is the sack in which you store your food supply. You should also put any scented items in it (toothpaste, baby powder, *etc.*) before hanging it in a tree each night before you sleep. Do not keep it in the tent with you as the scent will attract bears and other animals, and they may want to get in your tent (or take you out!) and have a little snack.

There are other methods for hanging a bear bag, but the PCT (Pacific Crest Trail) method with the clove hitch is the most common and is the one we used. Though not a complete overview, here are our bear bag hanging tips:

* Look for a branch on a tree at a 90° angle, about 20 feet up from the ground.

* It should hang so it is at least twelve feet off the ground, six feet out from the trunk, and six feet below the tree branch so that a bear cannot reach it from either the ground or the branch (if he climbs

out on the branch, lies down, and swipes his paws down below to try to get to it).

* Watch this video of the PCT bear bag method: https://youtu.be/GnQygS85Mxk.

* Throw your bear bag before dark. Sunsets would regularly set up the first part (throw the rope over the branch), so it was ready and waiting for us to clip the bags on once we were ready. The hardest part is finding the tree and throwing the rope over it.

* If you are short, it helps to stand on a slope or incline if you can find one nearby. This will help you tie the clove hitch higher and therefore raise the bag high enough from the ground.

For alternatives to bear bags, see Chapter II.

X. Loose Ends
~ *Sunsets*

Here we have a few misfit tips and tidbits that don't fit elsewhere in the book.

87. NO HANDS

When we first started our thru-hike, we were only a couple days in when we met a guy who I thought was extending his hand for me to shake, but when I looked down, his hand was in a tight fist formation. I was at a loss. Luckily, he was kind and must have seen "NEWBIE HIKER" written across my face and explained to me that this is what thru-hikers do instead of shaking hands. They fist bump.

The purpose of the fist bump is simply to not spread germs. Hikers do not get a chance to shower daily, and even though they take precautions and use hand sanitizer, it is not as effective in eliminating contaminants as soap and water are. Returning home from the trail, I was so accustomed to fist bumping that I would unintentionally offer my fist to a friend's open-handed shake.

Serious germ-a-phobes can always rely on the elbow bump, a much more advanced move, or not even touch at all and simply greet others verbally with no body parts.

88. FOOD SHARING

Along the same thought line as the fist bump is to not share food, as doing so can lead to intestinal problems for the entire camp. It's so easy to mess this up. We are taught at a young age that the way we demonstrate friendship is to share, and since food is a great way to build community, it is natural to share food. So, you offer your trail mix to other hikers in camp, they reach their tainted hands into your bag and *voilà*, everyone is on the quick weight-loss plan... as if hiking 20 miles a day wasn't taking off the weight fast enough.

Norovirus is one of the leading causes of illness along the trail. It is caused by unsanitary bathroom practices and is extremely contagious. The virus causes nausea, diarrhea, and a general malaise. The illness typically passes unaided in a couple of days, but infected individuals should see a doctor if the symptoms don't clear up. Because of some of the symptoms and the fact that hikers are, well, hiking, severe dehydration is a real possibility. Make sure you drink plenty of water.

In addition to not sharing food, and since noro is spread socially, many hikers choose to use their own pen when writing in shelter logs or to avoid the log all together.

89. LET'S TALK ABOUT SEX

What better tip to follow fist bumping and not sharing food to prevent germs than – sex! We mentioned in Chapter IV where not to have sex, but let's take a second to acknowledge that sex on the trail is a thing.

It's not a shock that many who share the daily struggles and joys of thru-hiking create a lasting bond, one that is sometimes romantic. On-trail romance is common and to be expected.

We, as a married couple, experienced a heightened libido and had some of the best sex of our 22 years of marriage. Strange, I know. After all, we didn't shower for days and were stinky most of the time. But being in nature each day and being in the best shape of our lives – had its effect.

Sex happens on the trail – in tents, in hammocks, in the woods (off the beaten path one would hope) and in hotels. Creativity can flourish as surroundings and cramped muscles dictate achievable positions.

And, as with so many other things, be aware when you are sharing space with others in order to minimize discomfort and awkward conversations later.

90. ALL IN THE TRAMILY

A majority of thru-hikers start the trail solo and, because hiking by oneself for 10+ hours a day can get lonely and monotonous, a trail family – in thru-hiker vernacular "tramily"– is often formed. These can be loose or tight-knit groups, but in general they look after members and provide camaraderie.

One of the dangers of the tramily is wanting to form one at the beginning too quickly. Trail families are great and many people have written fondly of their experiences with them causing new hikers to think, *hmmm, I'm going to get me one of them tramily things immediately.* This is invariably a mistake. The problem is, at the beginning, everyone is trying to figure out their pace and the type of hike (mileage, days off, *etc.*) that works best for them. Tramilies formed early often splinter quickly; slow members try to keep up with fast members and end up injured, some in the group want to hang out in town for a couple of days and some want to press on, or some want to do 10 mile days and others want to do 15.

Don't worry. You will find your group (if you want to). However, if you force it, you may find that you end up with a fractured group. It's almost inevitable that members of tramilies will be added and removed over the course of 2,200 miles, but the most change will be seen in those who form a bond early on.

91. HITCHIKING

Hitchhiking is one of those things that is weird (and even illegal in some states) in everyday life, but very common for hikers. It is also legal in all states on the AT except New York. Often you will need to hitch from the trail to town or to a hostel/hotel, restaurant or resupply. This was one of those things that I didn't care for, but I liked it better than having to pay for a shuttle. Every time we attempted a hitch, we got one, usually within 5-10 minutes. A few times we were walking towards a town and got a hitch without asking. For the most part, towns thrive on thru-hikers and the people are very helpful with rides and information.

When hitching, stand a good number of feet before a place where a car can pull over safely. Make it easy for the driver to pull out of traffic to stop and pick you up. Smile, but try not to look creepy. Some hikers do a dance or hold up a funny sign stating they are not a serial killer or the like.

If you are a guy, hitchhike with a girl! This quickly tells a driver "even though that scruffy-bearded guy looks rough, he must be OK because that cute girl is with him." It works (thanks, Chica!).

Once you get a ride, ask where the driver wants you. Some drivers don't want you in the front seat and some truck drivers only want you to ride in the truck-bed. If you are inside, immediately roll down the window… you stink. When the driver drops you off, it is goodwill to offer a couple of bucks for gas, though it is unusual for a driver to accept the money. One time, we insisted the driver take it because he was clearly in need and he helped us when we were in need.

92. WALK THIS WAY

The Appalachian Trail is well marked for most of the route. Even so, occasionally it is still easy to go off trail. It looks logical that the trail goes one way, when it really goes another. In these instances, hikers often lay downed tree limbs across the wrong path indicating you should go the other way. This tip is extremely helpful if you are aware of it.

Even knowing this, sometimes we walked right over tree branches because we felt that was naturally where the trail went, only to have the path peter out. We would pull out the GPS, see we were off and laugh as we stepped back over the limbs onto the correct trail.

93. STRAIGHT FROM HEAVEN

Occasionally, along your thru-hike you come across a person who helps you out in some way. Maybe it's giving you an ice-cold soda on a hot day after a hard climb; maybe it's a ride into town or a bandage right after you sliced your finger open. It might even be opening their home to provide you with a shower, a meal, or a bed. Whatever the situation, it's like they were meant to be there at that time. Trail angel is the perfect description for that person who gives their time, money, and effort to help thru-hikers when they need it most. And, also aptly named, trail magic is the name applied to the kindness the trail angel has bestowed.

Be grateful, non-expectant, and gracious whenever you meet one of these angels. You are doing nothing that deserves their kindness. They just are kick-ass people.

94. ELECTRONICS

Though thru-hiking the Appalachian Trail is the perfect situation to let go of some of the everyday electronics some of us are a bit too connected to, some modern-day devices serve you well. We used our iPhones for reading, listening to audio books and music, checking the weather, the Guthook's GPS app, and calling ahead for hostel reservations.

Cell phone coverage will be hit or miss on the Appalachian Trail. The overwhelming consensus of thru-hikers is that Verizon has the best coverage, so Verizon is what we used for our cell provider. Except for some spots on the trail where there are no carriers that have coverage – you ARE in the middle of the woods after all – we were very happy with the service.

For those of you who want to keep track of a family member or partner out on the trail, thru-hikers can choose from a variety of GPS tracking devices that attach easily to their backpacks (*i.e.*, the SPOT Gen3 Satellite GPS Messenger or the Garmin InReach Mini).

95. KEY SWAP

No, we're not talking about a 70s era swingers' party. Instead, key swap is a term used to describe a strategy for self slack-packing, which has multiple configurations but always includes at least one hiker and one vehicle.

Key swapping has its advantages. First, for hikers with a tight time frame, key swap allows them to hike with less gear, allowing them to hike faster and put in more miles. Secondly, the strategy means they have a warm dry place to sleep each night and costs for hostel or hotel stays are minimized. Finally, having constant access to a vehicle means easier access to towns and restaurants.

But key swapping has a couple of disadvantages as well. First, the key swapper misses out on some of the social interaction that takes place at shelters, tent sites, and hostels. Secondly, sometimes trailheads are not spaced in such a way that works for the slack-packer's schedule. The distance may be too short or too long for the day. Finally, those with a purist attitude might find the technique lacking as a full pack is not being used and the assistance of a vehicle is.

We saw a few people utilizing key swaps to thru-hike. Here are the two methods we saw in action:

1 Person, 2 Vehicles

It was only after meeting Doppler on three consecutive days that we stopped him and asked him just what the hell he was doing. We always seemed to run into him mid-day, yet he was hiking southbound while we were headed north.

"I use a motorcycle and truck to slack-pack. I drive my truck north and then hike south to the motorcycle. Then I drive the motorcycle north to my truck, and spend the night. Next morning, I leave the motorcycle behind and drive the truck to the next northern trailhead where I repeat the process – I hike back to my motorcycle and drive back to the truck."

The beauty of this system is that Doppler stored his motorcycle in the truck bed at night and slept in the back seat. Also, he did not have to depend on a second person.

2 People, 1 Vehicle

The true key-swap method is a strategy for two hikers. The first (Hiker 1) is dropped off further north along the trail where he/she will hike southbound. The second hiker (Hiker 2) drives south to the trailhead and parks the vehicle, then sets off northbound.

At some point the two hikers will cross paths. When they do, Hiker 2 will hand off the keys of the vehicle to Hiker 1. Once Hiker 1 reaches the end of the hike and the vehicle, he will drive north to pick up hiker 2.

96. LEAVE NO TRACE (LNT) PRINCIPALS

To protect all wilderness areas from deterioration due to the high use along the AT, the following Leave No Trace principles are encouraged. They are outlined briefly below and are self-explanatory (as well as self-regulating). For more information go to http://www.appalachiantrail.org.

* Plan ahead and prepare.
* Travel and camp on durable surfaces.
* Dispose of waste properly.
* Leave what your find.
* Minimize campfire impacts.
* Respect wildlife.
* Be considerate of other visitors.

XI. WHAT'S STOPPING YOU?
~ *Chica & Sunsets*

You would think that anyone who put so much effort, thought, money, research, and training into planning a six-month trip would almost certainly complete it. You might be surprised then that most hikers who set out to complete a thru-hike of the AT don't.

In fact, in 2017, *half* of the hikers who attempted a thru-hike dropped out by the mid-way point, and only about 25% completed the whole trail.

Quitting does not equal failure. Any time spent hiking the Appalachian Trail can be a positive, fulfilling experience. However, those who set out with the goal of completing the AT as a thru-hike certainly want to do it. Since forewarned is forearmed, we want to address the top reasons hikers quit the trail, so you will be equipped with as much information as possible.

We like to practice what we call the "positive power of negative thinking." This certainly helped us when we quit our corporate jobs, sold almost everything, and moved to Costa Rica, semi-retiring in our early 40s. After researching everything we could on Costa Rica, we imagined the worst-case scenarios that could happen when moving to and living in a foreign country. We then strategized on how we would react and cope to get through those situations, should they occur. Imagining the negatives and having a plan in place on how to handle almost anything empowered us with confidence that we would overcome any obstacles.

This same way of thinking helped us plan for the Appalachian Trail. For instance, we followed hikers on YouTube before we did our own thru-hike. When we saw most of them dropping out, we'd analyze what happened to them and talk about what we would do if faced with similar difficulties. We also read books and discussed topics in online forums, all the while keeping in mind all the stumbling blocks that might destroy our resolve and make us want to quit.

By envisioning the worst-case scenarios on the trail, we were able to talk about various plans of action. We hoped these tactics would get us over the hurdles when they occurred, and we could continue our hike. Some might call this being pessimistic; we call it being realistic. Just look at the completion rate! Know the risks and what can go wrong, be ready with your plan of action, and follow through accordingly. We want you guys to finish!

Let's look at the top five reasons why hikers quit their attempt of a thru-hike on the Appalachian Trail.

97. MONEY DRIES UP

Remember, we talked about money and budgeting in the beginning of this book (Chapter I), and this is why it's so important. It might seem obvious, but you wouldn't believe how many hikers drop out because they simply run out of money.

One reason is that some hikers don't think it all the way through or budget for the entire time they will be on the trail, thinking "I'll make it work with what I have."

Another reason is some of the younger (and sometimes not-so-young) hikers tend to party in the trail towns, and alcohol, especially when purchased at bars or restaurants, depletes a budget faster than just about anything. Also, a hangover the next morning doesn't bode well for a day of high-mileage hiking, so you might think, "Oh, I'll take another zero day," and end up spending even more money for an extra, unplanned night at a hostel.

And finally, one major reason hikers run out of money is they don't stick to their original plan. Even when you plan and budget carefully, you may discover you want your experience to be different.

You might not like hostels, for example, and you want to stay in hotels instead. You might not like hitchhiking, and therefore will choose to pay for shuttles or taxis. You might find you enjoy taking zeros in town and do more than you planned (how do you think our pal Zero Hero got his trail name?). Your cravings may take over, and you might reward yourself with beef jerky or Mountain House meals every day instead of Spam or ramen noodles. Whatever the reasons, I think you can understand how this could easily happen – as you don't know how you'll want to live until you are actually there in the woods.

There are two ways to budget for your thru-hike. One, hike the hike your money allows for. Two, decide on the ideal hike you want and save enough money for it. We recommend the latter, as it gives you the most flexibility and recipe for success.

98. LONELINESS

We've talked about tramilies and friendships, which are prevalent as tons of hikers are on the trail in the typical season (with numbers climbing each year). However, some hikers are loners, or they don't mesh with a tramily, or they might be lonely even though they are hiking with someone or with a group. Whatever the reason, some hikers become depressed and miss family, friends, or significant others from home.

Even though some hikers seek solitude, many eventually find that they long for some companionship. One way to combat loneliness is to stay at the shelters and campsites noted in the guidebook (instead of stealth sites all by yourself). This way, even if you hike alone during the day, you will be with other hikers at night to hang out and talk. Another way is to stay at hostels while in town (instead of a hotel room all by yourself) – hostels have that community feel with a kitchen, bunkrooms and great rooms. Sometimes nothing is better than to commiserate with other hikers about your body pain or a terrifying stretch of trail, or to share opinions on where the best place to eat is.

99. BOREDOM, NO FUN

Each day on the trail brings its own diverse array of terrain, animals, flowers, streams, rivers, vistas, and mountains. If you're lucky, you'll come across some trail magic, which brightens the spirit of any thru-hiker immensely. You sleep each night in a different location, see amazing sunsets and sunrises, interact with fellow hikers, several of whom end up becoming really good friends… how could this possibly be boring? Yet some hikers who quit claim they "just got bored" or "just weren't having fun anymore."

Think about walking 20 miles, day after day, for up to six months, sometimes in stifling heat, sometimes in the freezing cold, and other times in all-day rain. Honestly, does anyone do this in everyday life? Some AT hikers hike marathon distances (26.2 miles) or more, *every day*. It's not hard to understand how the "fun" might wear off, even in the natural beauty of the woods.

The best way to prevent boredom is to be prepared for it ahead of time. Have some ideas in place for when it happens so you can fight it. Sunsets and I would sometimes listen to music or audio books, discuss exciting plans for the future, or talk about how cool it was that we were on the Appalachian Trail and recap all we'd done already. The best thing that helped us was dreaming out loud and picturing the finish line (Katahdin).

100. INJURY / ILLNESS

Getting injured is a distinct possibility if you attempt a thru-hike. Most hikers get some type of injury, such as a sprained ankle, knee injury, plantar fasciitis, foot stress fracture, a broken bone, *etc.*

One hiker we knew, Papa John, started the trail with

his spouse, but early on she tripped and took a nosedive – falling flat on her face on a rock. She was immediately taken out of the game. In fact, she still has some lingering issues. He went home with her for a couple of weeks, but then she convinced him to get back on the trail without her. He finished a day after us on Katahdin.

We worried that an injury would take us off the trail. I mean, how do you avoid getting injured? We tried to be careful with where we stepped and how fast we went down steep descents, and most of the time, we kept our eyes glued to our feet. Though our trekking poles saved us many times, we still tripped and fell almost daily with seemingly no way to prevent it. We had "baby" injuries that bothered us (foot, ankle, and knee pain), but fortunately nothing major enough to go to a doctor or to take us off trail.

101. FAMILY EMERGENCY

Yes, an extra tip. It's unfortunate, but it happens. A family member back home has an accident, is diagnosed with an illness, or worst of all, dies. These sudden emergencies may derail or interrupt your plans, but of course, family is far more important than hiking the trail. The trail will always be there, your family may not.

On the flip side, happy events *are* planned (births,

weddings, graduations, *etc.*), and many hikers will take some days off to attend such an event and then get back on the trail.

102. TOO HARD

Some hikers simply find the physical demands too difficult to continue, and like those who find it boring, these hikers think it is just not fun anymore.

The Appalachian Trail is not the proverbial "walk in the park." The trail is quite challenging. In fact, it is much more difficult today than when the AT was first born. When Earl Shaffer became the first person to thru-hike the AT, he found it much more level – on roads, through farms and rolling valleys, over even paths through the woods – not the crazy mountain ascents and descents we have today.

We definitely had our individual good and bad days, but one thing we agreed on is that almost every single day on the Appalachian Trail was. Just. Plain. HARD. It could be the weather one day. Or a certain mountain. Or a hurt foot or leg. But no matter what, it seemed that every single day had its difficulties. We will both tell you – the AT is the most ambitious and most demanding experience we've ever had.

All of these daily challenges can adversely affect thru-hikers at one time or another on their journey.

For some, it overtakes them and they decide the need to stop hiking is more important than the need to continue. Being mentally ready for a thru-hike is just as important as being physically prepared.

By the time we started our thru-hike, we were completely determined and focused. We knew that 75% of all hikers quit, and we knew all the reasons why. We knew that, barring a severe injury or family emergency, nothing was going to stop us from obtaining our goal of summiting Mt. Katahdin.

We sometimes find it impossible to believe that we actually did it! It was a magical, challenging, rewarding, and life-changing experience. Sometimes it seems like a dream.

A REALLY, REALLY GOOD DREAM.

CLOSING

For those about to walk, we salute you.

Dear prospective thru-hiker,

Months before we set off on Springer Mountain, we prepped the standard way pre-thru-hikers do. We were active on Facebook groups and forums. We spewed stats to anyone who would listen about our well-researched but barely used gear. And we installed the obligatory countdown app on our iPhones and waited for the proverbial water to boil.

With all our gear purchased, we took a three-day backpacking trip, in the rain no less, to *shake down* that gear. That trip represented the longest consecutive-nights backpacking trip either of us had ever made, and we were about to spend six months outside! We were not alone. According to the website *The Trek* (https://thetrek.co/appalachian-trail/2017-appalachian-trail-thru-hiker-survey-general-hiker-stats), the stats for our thru-hiking class (2017) show 76% of respondents had spent seven or fewer consecutive nights on a trail… ever.

So, we were green. And we weren't in the best shape of our lives either, using only a daily walk on a treadmill to get us through the harsh Wisconsin winter. We started a YouTube channel and, though no one mentioned it at the time, there was widespread doubt among our viewers that we would be able to endure 2,189.8 miles up and over the mountains of 14 states.

Against whatever the odds of not completing a thru-hike, we did persevere. We summited Mt. Katahdin, Maine, 179 days after setting off from Springer Mountain, Georgia. Truth be told, we started from the approach trail, adding nine miles that didn't count to our trek.

Knowing what we know now as successful thru-hikers, what advice would we give to those about to embark on the journey of a lifetime?

Grab Your Shovel

Most of the advice we are about to lay on you is designed to be considered before you leave and within the first month of your trip. After 30 days on the trail you will have most, if not all, of the knowledge you will need to be a long-distance hiker because, by then, you *are* one. So, before you get on the trail, take all advice from anyone with a shovelful of salt. Eat the meat, spit out the bone.

You may have seen the meme quoting the poet and mystic, Rumi:

"When setting out on a journey, do not seek advice from someone who never left home."

Now this may sound harsh, but many of the people offering advice have never left home, or more accurately, have never backpacked for a long distance. Ironically (or is it hypocritically?), before we left on our thru-hike, we spoke with authority on many subjects we thought we knew about because, you know, we had read about them.

Everyone wants to help, but when we commiserate with other members of our hiking class, we can spread misinformation among ourselves. The blind are leading the blind with questions like: "What sleeping bag are y'all taking? What stove? What pack? What tent?" You *will* get answers because your inexperienced *compadres* know everything about their gear… except how it will operate over six months of abuse.

And they can't wait to tell you all about what they have learned.

And we're not done with that salt. The same holds true for the well-traveled soul, so keep this saying in mind: *Your Mileage May Vary*. And it will. One person's joy with a tent will be another's bane. One hiker swears by hiking boots and another by trail runners (that would be us). They can *both* be right.

And since we are on a roll with platitudes, let's add this one for good measure:

Trust, but verify.

Know Thyself

The more you know about how you tick, the more likely you are to succeed. For example, we knew, barring injury or a family emergency, we would complete the trail. We did not share the incredulousness of our YouTube subscribers or that of some of our family.

We are a tenacious couple. If we decide we are going to do something, we almost always accomplish it. That comes with being married for 22 years and already doing things outside the norm. Like quitting our jobs in 2013 to move to Costa Rica to live on less and to hold adventure above wealth or accumulation. Like becoming successful authors, even though writing was neither of our vocations.

We know our strengths and weaknesses individually and as a couple. For example, we knew Sunsets was susceptible to heat exhaustion and that we would have to deal with that in the summer. We knew that Chica feared a possible bear encounter.

We also knew what we didn't know, mostly related

to gear and outdoor skills. By acknowledging what was missing in our mental tool bag, we were able to research, learn, practice, and add strength to our skillset. Admitting you are in over your head allows you to do something about it. If, instead, you say, "I got this," without ever coming to terms with your lack of knowledge, skill, or determination, then you are setting yourself up for failure or possible injury.

Finally, understand why thru-hikers quit. We spelled it out in the previous chapter, but combine that information with what you know about yourself. Do you lack self-control when it comes to money? Do you get bored easily, or will you be lonely without constantly being around others? Once again, acknowledge your weakness, own it, then control your destiny. The next two points are going to expand on two of the reasons hikers quit.

Don't Get Injured

Easier said than done, right? Sort of. Although you could fall and break a bone or sprain an ankle, those aren't the most common injuries that take trekkers off the trail. The injuries that are most likely going to end your hike are foot injuries, including blisters and overuse injuries. These types of ailments can be debilitating. The worst part is they are more likely to happen in the beginning miles of your journey and can destroy your will for completing the rest of the hike.

We remember rolling into Poplar Stamp tent site, a few days from Springer Mountain. The camp was filled with hikers nursing messed up feet. They proudly showed off their battle wounds while bemoaning the following day's hike. At least two of the five in camp that day didn't make it past North Carolina.

The good news is, to a large extent, these injuries can be avoided. Our number one tip for foot and overuse prevention?

Start slowly,
be methodical in your early mileage,
and resist the temptation to go big early.

Beginning the Appalachian Trail is like participating in a big race. So much excitement, energy, and adrenalin makes it difficult to control yourself. But believe me, even if you can hack it from a cardiovascular standpoint, your feet and legs cannot. Oh, they will soldier on because you are requiring it of them, but they will betray you, suddenly, at some point. A person cannot suddenly go from walking a couple of flat miles a day to lumbering up and down mountains for 15 or 20 miles over eight to ten hours.

Writing out a plan will help you keep your mileage in check and help minimize injuries. Our plan was simple: limit mileage to eight miles a day (with one day off) for the first week, ten miles a day for the second week (with a zero day), 12 miles the next, then 14, but we added an extra week of 12-mile days, as our bodies told us we weren't ready. Just as important as having a plan is listening to your body when it is telling you the plan needs to be revised. By the time we got to mid-Virginia (six weeks in), we were strong and healthy and able to bust out those big miles hikers always brag about. If we had tried a 14-mile day too early, we could have easily been injured and demoralized.

All in the Family

As you prepare for a thru-hike, inevitably you may get some wrong ideas. Or maybe not wrong ideas, but the wrong timing. Let us explain. If you are like most hikers planning to hike the length of the Appalachian Trail, you won't actually have access to the trail, nor will you have the time to hike 10 hours a day multiple times a week. So, you read, you watch YouTube videos, and you participate in question/answer sessions on social media.

All of this information is great, but it may lead you to false conclusions. For example, we read over and over again how ravenous thru-hikers can get. It's true. However, something that is rarely mentioned is that hiking hunger doesn't usually makes its appearance for a long time. For us it was about three weeks before it set in. But (here's the rub) we each packed about four pounds of unnecessary food for our first four days on the trail because we thought we would be starving.

In a similar vein is the trail family, the group you connect with that helps each other through thick mud and thin, with moral support and by lending a helping hand. You share gear, space, and food. You experience the trail together and forge lasting bonds.

Once again, the problem is a wonderful part of the trail has been described to you, but the timing has not. Trail families build, fracture, and recompose during the long trek of a thru-hike. Those who force a trail family early will be forced to speed up or slow down to match pace with the pack, and as mentioned above, this is a recipe for an injury pie. Our advice – don't worry about building a tramily. It will occur naturally as commonality is found with pace, personality, and goals.

Last But Not Least

We'd like to leave you with several helpful, commonly stated maxims.

Don't quit on a bad day. You will put a great amount of resources into thru-hiking the Appalachian Trail. The trail requires large commitments, both in time spent preparing and actually hiking as well as a monetary investment for gear and supplies to sustain you over the five to seven months you spend on the trail. Do not throw it all away because you've spent three days straight walking in the rain. Stop, take some time in town and dry out. Have a beer and a burger. But, do *not* quit on a bad day. If it's a great day and you think completing the trail is not something you really want to do, no problem. But we humans tend to think short term and can make poor decisions when we are miserable. By the way, you *will* have miserable days on the trail. That's why you will often hear, "No pain, no rain, no Maine."

Stop and pick those blackberries. Or swim in that lake. Or take the "blue blaze" (a short trail off of the AT) to the fire tower. Here's a secret: Mt. Katahdin will be there if you are a day or two off schedule… or even a month. Sunsets really wished we had stopped to swim in this one lake in Maine. The two weeks previous had been too cold for swimming. But on this day, it was 80 degrees, and there was a perfect beach and we were hot and stinking from four days without a shower. We didn't stop because we were trying to make time and miles. Ugh. We still regret that decision.

Take more pictures of people! We heard this before we set off and still wish we had taken more. As a pair, we are somewhat introverted but were surprised at how many friends and great social experiences we had on our trek. And we didn't take enough of those types of pictures. You will naturally take the scenic shots, or maybe get some animals, but don't forget to capture your friends' images too.

******

Thru-hiking the Appalachian Trail can restore one's faith in humanity and can be life-affirming and life-altering, all in the best ways imaginable. It may seem overwhelming, but with proper planning and determination, your journey of over 2,000 miles can be a reality. It begins simply with your first step on the trail.

BONUS – GEAR LISTS

I. Chica's & Sunsets' Gear List

To give you a full account of our gear, we will describe and detail the advantages and disadvantages of each piece, giving our opinions with the following scale: LOVED, LIKED, HATED, MEH.

We will start with our shared gear, which only one of us carried but both benefited from or used, then go over our individual gear. Our base weights (not including food and water) were 16 pounds (Chica) and 18 pounds (Sunsets).

SHARED GEAR

TENT (LOVED) – Big Agnes Copper Spur UL 3. The BA was an excellent choice for us and we used it the whole trip. We're happy we went with it rather than our second choice, the Zpacks Triplex, for the primary reasons that the BA was dual-walled, could be freestanding, and costs about $500 less. The only advantage of the Zpacks was it was about three pounds lighter. With us sharing weight, a small weight penalty was no big deal.

The tent held up well in high winds and rain, and on pleasant nights we could leave the fly off and sleep under the stars. It had two entrances/vestibules so we didn't have to crawl over each other to get in or out and could store our gear separately. The Big Agnes fit Sunsets' 6'3" frame comfortably (with two inches to spare at bottom and top). The shelter was downright palatial.

Our only complaint was with Big Agnes customer service. Many of our friends had great experiences; we didn't. Our request was simple – a tree branch had fallen on our tent during the night and we needed a replacement segment to the pole system. We even told them it wasn't a warranty issue and were happy to pay. It took a couple of days shy of a full month to get a replacement segment – and this is while we were out hiking the AT. We were in the wilderness in a compromised tent – not exactly a comfortable way to sleep.

So, BA Tent Score: 5 Twinkling Stars. BA Customer Service: 1 Withering Star. 1 Star because we did talk to a live person, we could understand them, and they had a nice demeanor. Despite the service issue, we recommend the tent highly, especially if you are a couple; it is roomy and reliable.

TENT FOOTPRINT (LIKED) – Tyvek. We bought a piece of Tyvek that was cut for the Copper Spur 3. It had grommets and worked well enough. We bought it from ebay and it lasted the entire trip.

Here's a tip for Tyvek – wash it several times in a washing machine prior to use and air dry to make the material soft and the crinkly sound will go away (mostly).

The Big Agnes tent has a delicate floor, so a footprint is advisable. BA sells one, but it costs about $60 ($20 for the Tyvek) and is only a bit lighter than the Tyvek.

WINDOW INSULTATION KIT (LIKED) – We bought the insulation kit for the thin plastic sheet it contained. Purpose? To help the loud rustling noise of the Therm-a-Rest NeoAir XLite air mattresses we both had. Placed under our pads, the plastic reduced the noise noticeably. It was strong, packed down small, and weighed almost nothing.

LINELOC 3 (LOVED) – Zpacks.com Guy-Line Adjusters. These make setting up the fly fast. After staking out, just pull on the paracord and the line lock holds the position for a tight pitch.

CARBON TENT STAKES (HATED) – Zpacks (6.4"). Not one in eight lasted a month on the AT. An expensive item for very little weight savings. We ended up replacing them with $0.49 Walmart stakes, which also bent but did not break. Also, people leave tent stakes at campsites all the time, so it is easy to pick up a spare.

POOPER SCOOPER (LOVED) – A 9" aluminum snow tent stake worked great for digging our 6" deep cat hole. We wrapped paracord around the handle which made it more comfortable while digging. Some will try to convince you that a trowel is unnecessary. Try digging a 6" inch cat hole with your boot heel or a stick.

STOVE (LOVED) – MSR PocketRocket. This worked great, it was small and light and heated water pretty quickly. NOTE: we sent our cook stove and pots home about halfway through our hike. We found that we were both too tired at the end of hiking all day to cook. Plus it was summer and the last thing we wanted to do was eat a hot meal.

BEAR BAG HANGING KIT (LOVED) – Zpacks.

FIRST AID (MEH) – Included Band-Aids, Neosporin, Leukotape, Benadryl, KT Tape, Vaseline, Vitamin I (ibuprophen), sewing kit, safety pins, and nail clippers.

4-PORT USB WALL CHARGER (LOVED) – This plugged into a wall outlet and had 4 USB ports, so we could plug in both our phones and our battery chargers (4 devices) all at once.

ULTRAPOD TREE WRAP AND TRIPOD (LOVED) – This works as a tripod and also has a Velcro strip that can wrap around trees, poles, *etc.* Great for timed pictures in the middle of the woods.

DAYPACK (LOVED) – Sea to Summit Ultra-Sil. This daypack was the bomb – so lightweight and it folded to the size of a hacky-sack. We used it in town or when we slack-packed.

AWOL'S *GUIDE* (LOVED) – *The A.T. Guide Northbound 2017* by David "Awol" Miller. We kept a small notebook and pen in the ziplock bag that came with it from Awol's website. We had our local print shop cut the spine and coil-bind it for us.

INSECT REPELLENT/SUNSCREEN (MEH) – DEET and sunscreen (various brands). Both worked how they were supposed to work.

SAWYER BACK FLUSH COUPLING (LOVED) – Gear that facilitates multiple uses is good gear. The coupling allows you to backflush the Sawyer Water Filtration System without using the bulky, heavy syringe included. The coupling also allows you to set up a hands-free gravity feed.

CHICA'S (UNSHARED) GEAR

PACK

BACKPACK (LOVED) – Osprey Aura AG 50. I actually trained with the Osprey Exos 48 before the AT and started having severe hip pain about a week before our start date. A friend came through, who happened to have a new Aura AG 50 available that I could try – and it was love at first fitting! This pack is made for a woman, has an all-in-one-piece hip belt with padding (and extenders for the front of your hips that you can adjust when you lose weight). Super-efficient ventilation system on the back. I loved everything about this pack. The best part was it hardly felt like I had anything on my back most days.

TRASH COMPACTOR BAG (LOVED) – Some hikers also used a contractor garbage bag; both work the same as a heavy-duty plastic waterproof bag. It lined the inside of my backpack and waterproofed the contents – worked great – nothing ever got wet inside. One lasted me my whole thru-hike.

PACK COVER (LIKED) – Sea to Summit. A cover was necessary when it was raining, but the top didn't work great after a while and the top brain part of my backpack would always get wet.

SLEEP SYSTEM

SLEEPING QUILT (LOVED) – Enlightened Equipment Revelation (10°F, regular width, extra-long – so I could easily pull it over my head on cold nights). The concept of a quilt sounds odd, but it worked well for me. The back part is open (like a regular quilt) because studies have shown that when you lie on top of a blanket, the fill underneath you is compressed and doesn't help keep you warm anyway. The quilt cinches around your feet and has straps that attach to your sleeping pad, and you can also cinch and snap around your neck or over your head to keep out cold air. On warm nights, you can un-cinch everything, and it lies flat like a blanket (to kick off easily).

SLEEPING BAG LINER (LOVED) – Sea to Summit Thermolite Reactor. This was great; it adds 15°F warmth or I used it by itself in the summer. I also used it as a "fitted sheet" to put around my air mattress in summer when it was hot. It put a layer between my sweaty, stinky body and the mattress, and I threw it in the wash when in town.

AIR MATTRESS (LOVED) – Therm-a-Rest NeoAir XLite (women's regular). So many good reviews call this mattress the most comfortable, lightweight and insulated option. It made sleeping in the woods each night as comfortable as I was going to get. It was a bit loud until we started using the window insulation kit.

PILLOW (LOVED) – Big Sky DreamSleeper UltraLight. For an inflatable pillow, this is the cat's meow. I'm a two-pillow sleeper and this still worked for me. Comfortable and high enough, and when deflated it took up very little space. I liked putting my buff over it as a pillowcase.

SIT PAD (LOVED) – Therm-a-Rest Z Seat. I used this little accordion fold-up seat rest during the day to sit on if the ground or log was wet, and I used it in camp as a doormat by the door of my tent.

FOOD/WATER SYSTEM

SPORK (LOVED) – Sea to Summit Long Handle Titanium. It was sturdy and never broke; I loved the long handle for digging deep into peanut butter jars and Mountain House meals.

TOWEL (LIKED) – ShamWow. It worked OK for anything from wiping down the tent after a rainstorm to drying my body after a swim.

COOK POT (LOVED) – Toaks Titanium (750 mL). I bought some plastic tubing from a hardware store to wrap around the handles and the pull-tab on the lid so I could touch it without burning myself.

WATER BLADDER (LOVED) – Evernew Water Carry 2L. This is used to collect dirty water before filtering. The Evernew worked so much better than the ones that came with the Sawyer Squeeze (they were small and not durable) or another brand of 2L bladder we had tried (the filter screwed onto the bladder, but not perfectly, allowing some "dirty" water to leak out – not good). The Evernew is strong and hardy – lasted our whole thru-hike. Incidentally, we cut the bladder that came with the Sawyer and used it as a scoop to get water when needed.

WATER FILTER (LOVED) – Sawyer Squeeze. This worked great! Back flushed only two or three times on whole thru-hike. See this for detailed information on how the Squeeze works: https://appalachiantrailtales.com/sawyer-squeeze-filter-info.

HINT: When temps get around freezing, put the filter in your sleeping bag so it doesn't freeze; if it freezes, it is not noticeable in any way – but your water will not be filtered properly.

FOOD DRY BAG (LOVED) – Zpacks. It worked great – kept our food dry even when it poured all night.

ELECTRONICS

CELL PHONE, CHARGER, HEADPHONES (LOVED) – iPhone 7 Plus (256GB). It took awesome pictures and videos and had all the storage I needed; I never had to delete photos.

HEADLAMP (LIKED) – Black Diamond ReVolt. This came with rechargeable batteries, but they did not work well after the first charging, so I ended up using new non-rechargeable batteries, which worked fine.

CHARGER (LOVED) – Anker PowerCore 20100. This worked great in the woods to charge my phone every night. It could charge my iPhone 7 Plus five full times, and I would charge the Anker when in town.

CLOTHING

PUFFY JACKET (LOVED) – Mountain Hardwear Ghost Whisperer (down fill 800). It packed down to the size of a hand, was very lightweight, kept me warm on cold nights, and was quite comfortable.

FLEECE HOODIE (LOVED) – Cuddl Duds (half-zip). One of my favorite pieces of gear! Thinner than a fleece jacket, it takes off the chill but is not too warm. I wore it all the time and loved the hood, the longer length (to the lower hip) and the thumb-holes.

HIKING T-SHIRT (LOVED) – Icebreaker (women's). Merino wool is the best, and this was super lightweight with a low stink factor. It dried super-fast and felt great on.

SHORTS (LOVED) – Athleta Running Shorts. These were so comfortable – they prevented inner-thigh chafing and didn't ride up on me.

LEGGINGS (LOVED) – Athleta. These were very comfortable to wear when it was cold, either to hike or sleep in. They held up well.

BRA (LOVED) – Smartwool (merino wool). Quick-drying and super comfy (sometimes I even slept in it!).

UNDERWEAR (LOVED) – ExOfficio Give-N-Go Sport Mesh Hipkini. This underwear was very breathable and this style didn't ride up on me, staying perfectly in place (even for a quick dip in a lake).

LINER SOCKS, 2 pairs (LOVED) – Injinji Toesock Liners. See more information in Chapter V.

HIKING SOCKS, 2 pairs (LOVED) – Darn Tough Light Hiker Micro Crew. See more information in Chapter V.

HIKING SHOES (LOVED) – Salomon Women's X-Mission 3 W (went through 3 pairs on trail). See more details in Chapter V.

CAMP SHOES (LOVED) – Xero Z-Trails. These sandals were super lightweight, flat, and comfy in town or camp. They strap on tightly for safe water crossings.

BUFF (LOVED) – Several options; check out buffusa.com. One of my favorite pieces of gear – I used it every night as a pillow case over my inflatable pillow and most days to keep hair out of my eyes, to cover up oily hair, and to keep sun off my head. I could also pull it down to cover my ears when cold.

SLEEPWEAR/TOWNWEAR (LOVED). REI wool socks, Athleta skort, Icebreaker merino wool T-shirt.

WATCH (LOVED) – Timex Ironman Triathlon. I've had this watch for a while and just love it.

GLOVES (LIKED) – Zpacks Possomdown. These were OK and kept the chill off. For winter weather though, you need something warmer. They will shrink in the dryer.

CYCLING SLEEVES (LOVED) – Cheap cycling

sleeves from Amazon with thumbholes. On cool mornings, I wore these with my T-shirt, and when it warmed up, I peeled them off without stopping or taking off my backpack. This was the best idea I had! Buffusa.com now makes cycling sleeves too.

GAITERS (LOVED) – Ultra Gam on Etsy. I really enjoyed having gaiters. They kept dirt and debris out of my shoes, and the design was colorful and cute to boot. I received compliments on these all the time.

BEANIE HAT (LOVED) – Choucas (choucashats.com). This kept my head warm and I love all the colors and designs they have.

SUN HAT (LOVED) – ExOfficio BugsAway. The hat was pretreated with permethrin and had a bendable brim and a chin cord to keep the hat secure.

MOSQUITO HEAD NET (LOVED) – Walmart (under $2!). I didn't love this for how it looked, but for the purpose of keeping swarming mosquitos off my face and out of my ears. I liked using it over my sun hat as the brim on the sun hat kept the net from touching my face, which is more annoying than you'd think.

CLOTHES DRY BAG (LOVED) – Zpacks.

RAIN JACKET (LOVED) – Patagonia Torrentshell

(women's). It kept me dry from rain (won't mention sweat), had long pit zips, a longer length just past hips, and I loved the adjustable hood.

OTHER

TREKKING POLES (LOVED) – LEKI Corklite SpeedLock. I liked how these poles collapsed and elongated. They are very secure, and I cannot tell you how many times my poles saved me from falling on my face or butt!

UMBRELLA (LOVED) – Zpacks Liteflex. I loved having an umbrella to keep rain off my face, head and top of my backpack. I worked out a system where I put the shaft under my backpack's chest strap and then hooked the bottom loop of the handle around my hip belt before closing – it kept the umbrella secure so I could use my hands for my trekking poles.

READING GLASSES (MEH) – I need glasses to read, so these were a must-have. I wrapped them with a small cloth and a rubber band for storage in the brain of my backpack; they never got crushed or broken.

PEE RAG (LOVED) – A cotton bandana worked well for me. See Chapter VII for more information.

CHILL RAG / COOLING TOWEL (LOVED) – A towel that you dip in water, wring out and swirl in the air to cool it. It works great if you put it around your neck, head, or wherever you are hottest. You can re-swirl to cool it down until it eventually dries.

SNOT/SWEAT RAG (LOVED) – Runningluv. This has elastic loops to wear on your hand and wrap around your wrist, but I just clipped it to the shoulder strap of my backpack. I used it to wipe my nose after "snot-rocketing" (blowing your nose naturally in the woods with no Kleenex). You can also use it for sweat.

POCKET KNIFE (LOVED) – Mini Swiss Army. I used this mainly for the scissors (which amazingly I needed all the time – duct tape, Leukotape, *etc.*).

EAR PLUGS (LIKED) – Flents Contour. These worked OK. I think my ears are unusual because about halfway through the night, the plugs would always fall out no matter what brand I tried. Ear plugs are a must for hostels, shelters or even tents (close to other tents) to block out snoring and other noise.

TOILETRIES – Toilet paper, wet wipes, hand sanitizer, tampons, brush, toothbrush, toothpaste, Carmex lip balm, small mirror, tweezers, and razor.

WATER BOTTLE HOLDER (LOVED) – Handmade by Justin Anderson (https://www.etsy.com/shop/JustinsUL). This holder keeps your bottle handy by attaching to the shoulder strap of your backpack – no struggling to reach the back side pocket of your pack, which is a surprisingly common problem with many packs.

WALLET (LOVED) – Zpacks (zip-pouch wallet). Small and waterproof, it was just as big as it needed to be for a few credit cards and cash.

PHONE HOLDER (LOVED) – Zpacks. This phone holder attached to the shoulder strap of my backpack and kept my cell phone handy. It has a front mesh pocket where I kept my sanitizer and lip balm.

SUNSETS' (UNSHARED) GEAR

PACK

BACKPACK (MEH) – Gossamer Gear Mariposa (60L). If you read reviews on the Mariposa, you will see that my rating is a dissenting one. Let me explain. The backpack is well-made, light and durable, and it has pockets in all the right places. It has a replaceable hip belt, so when you lose 50 pounds (like I did), you don't have to ditch the backpack all together.

So, what's the problem? The pack caused me shoulder pain. Not every day, not all day, but enough to make me notice it was a problem. I heard the same shoulder pain complaint from other Mariposa users. They were all tall with long torsos, like me. I give the pack 3 Stars. It may work for you, but this is my experience.

Gossamer Gear's customer service was almost flawless… almost. I contacted them three times. Two times they were unbelievably great. I had to buy a new hip belt and trying to pinpoint the next town was difficult. The customer service agent was able to tell me the exact delivery dates to help me get the belt in a timely manner. The second positive experience was when I stepped on my pack buckle and destroyed it. I contacted Gossamer Gear and the agent said he knew navigating their menu on a phone was a challenge, so he would send one for free. I found one at an outfitter in the next town (for $2) so it was a no-go, but the gesture was appreciated.

What was the request that wasn't handled perfectly? I'm glad you asked. Before getting on the trail, when I first bought the pack, I contacted the company asking about a pack cover. The conversation went something like this:

Me: I notice on your website you don't sell pack covers. Is the Mariposa waterproof or do I need a cover?

Customer Service: You should ask other hikers what they think.

I couldn't even think of a response, so I said thanks and goodbye. So odd.

PACK COVER (LIKED) – Zpacks. It worked OK. Due to the Mariposa's lid design, the top still got wet but would have with any other pack cover as well.

<u>SLEEP SYSTEM</u>

SLEEPING QUILT (LIKED) – Enlightened Equipment Revelation

(20° quilt). I chose a quilt over a traditional

"mummy" sleeping bag for several reasons. First – when I thought I had to count every ounce – was the weight savings.

The second advantage is for the person who tosses and turns in their sleep – aka, me. I can sleep on my back, my left side, my right side, and my belly all within an hour. A sleeping bag doesn't allow for that much movement. The quilt is designed to be strapped down to the sleeping pad. I almost never did this. In addition to multiple sleeping positions, I like to kick a leg out… or kick the whole quilt off. I sleep warm.

The 20-degree version worked fine but was not enough warm enough a few times and was too warm many times in the summer. That being said, I wasn't about to buy two separate quilts; suffer over spend, that's me.

Enlightened Equipment makes a quality product. And it's cool to customize the color and fill (I chose black and orange with 850 DownTek treated fill). They take a long time for custom orders, so order well in advance or buy one that is premade. For custom orders, I would add a couple weeks onto what they tell you the lead time is. I got mine extra long and extra wide. The added length allowed me to fully cover my head on cold nights. The size worked great for me and it still stuffed down to the size of a basketball.

AIR MATTRESS (LIKED) – Therm-a-Rest NeoAir XLite Sleeping Pad. Other than the name being excruciatingly long and hard to remember, I have no complaints about the NeoAir. If I had to do it all over, I would probably just get the torso-length version, as I propped my feet up on my backpack each night inside the tent rendering the extra length useless.

PILLOW (LOVED) – Big Sky International DreamSleeper UltraLight. First, I tried to use my clothes stuff sack as a pillow because of the weight (about 2 ounces) of a pillow. I even bought the Zpacks stuff sack that could be reversed, leaving a soft felted sleep surface. Lipstick on a pig I tell you. Along with NOT cutting your toothbrush down, investing in a pillow is the best weight ever spent. If you go with the Big Sky pillow, order well before your trip. The company does a great job of not keeping up with demand and the pillow is often out of stock, both on Amazon and the Big Sky International website.

FOOD/WATER SYSTEM

WATER FILTER (LOVED) – Sawyer Squeeze. The best gear are those things that work. That is what the Sawyer filter does.

WATER BLADDER (LOVED) – Evernew (2L). The Evernew fits the Sawyer perfectly and it is built to withstand the abuse of daily use.

WATER BOTTLES, 2 (LOVED) – Glaceau Smartwater (1L). Reusing these worked well for storing our clean water. Once they got too dirty, they were easily replaced and could be bought at any convenience store.

WATER BOTTLE HOLDER (LOVED). If it weren't for Chica, I would have never even thought about storing my Smartwater bottle anywhere but the hard-to-reach side pocket. Luckily, she saw a post on a Facebook group from a guy who was custom making 1-liter holders that attached to a backpack's shoulder strap and we ordered two. The accessory became one of our favorites. Like all great products, it solves a problem (hard-to-reach water bottles), it's built well (lasted our entire trip), and it's incredibly light. Plus, we love helping cottage industry pioneers. Buy yours from Justin Anderson's Etsy Shop: https://www.etsy.com/shop/JustinsUL.

FOOD DRY BAG (LIKED) – Zpacks Bear Bag. Expensive but effective. One shelter did have bear boxes that were bear-proof but not rodent-proof and an industrious band of rodents gnawed into every single bag in the box (always read shelter logs!). So, it's a good idea to have a repair kit along if you buy the Zpacks kit.

Also, once we hit Pennsylvania, I had to replace the 50 feet of paracord. It had become frayed and weak from use. One last tip – use a full size carabiner for your bear bag, not the mini size that Zpacks gives you.

SPOON (LIKED) – Sea to Summit Long Handled Spoon. Get the aluminum version and save a buck over a titanium spork. You need the long handle to dig deep down into the peanut butter jar. In my opinion the fork part is useless, so just go with a spoon.

COOK POT (LIKED) – Evernew (0.9L titanium). Lightweight and large enough for a big meal. The handles are coated with plastic so you can actually use them while cooking, unlike some other popular pots (I'm looking at you Toaks).

ELECTRONICS

CELL PHONE (LOVED) – iPhone 7 Plus (256GB). The iPhone acted as my video camera, digital camera, iPod, and ebook reader. We even used it to make phone calls once or twice. The large storage capacity meant very little time was used dealing with storage issues. The image stabilization is spectacular.

CHARGER (LIKED) – Anker PowerCore II 20000. This was total overkill as Chica and I each carried one. We filmed and did work on our phones daily... Okay, Chica filmed and worked on her phone daily. I read and listened to music. Still, we wanted to be sure we could stay powered up if we were on the trail for six or seven days straight. It's a great battery and can charge an iPhone 7 Plus about five times.

HEADLAMP (LIKED) – Black Diamond ReVolt. I know I am in the minority – the very very small minority – but I hardly used my headlamp at all. I did use the flashlight on my phone quite a bit. When I did use it, the ReVolt worked fine for me.

CLOTHING

We sent most of our clothing to Insect Shield (InsectShield.com) to be treated with permethrin. Ticks were not a problem for us on the trail; I credit Insect Shield. In six months between Chica and I, we had three ticks crawling on us and one that was attached. Not bad, I think.

SHORTS (LOVED) – The North Face. These shorts were shredded by the end of the hike so I threw them out. Too bad, as The North Face no longer makes them. They had a 9" inseam and a liner making underwear unnecessary.

T-SHIRTS, 2 (LOVED) – Icebreaker (merino wool). I am a very frugal shopper, yet I bought a T-shirt that retails for $80 (but at a whopping sale price of $40 – for a damn T-shirt!).

Still, I love them. Merino wool really does exhibit the properties it claims. It wicks sweat, holds in heat and cools when needed, sheds water, dries fast, and doesn't stink ... as bad as synthetic. It's a magical material.

TOWN SHIRT (MEH) – Walmart (tank top). In the summer I was always hot, so I bought this for $5.

CONVERTIBLE PANTS (LOVED) – REI. I thought I would hike in long pants. I never did. I did use the pants for town-wear and when we were doing laundry. I tried multiple pants and the REI ones worked the best. All the other brands I tried, Prana, *etc.*, had the zipper falling right on my knee cap. It rubbed when I walked and would have been problematic for a thru.

BUFF (LOVED). If you don't know what a buff is, you need to look it up. I used it around my wrist to wipe sweat from my brow, as a headband, around my neck when it was cold out, like a bank robber's mask, and I am sure a few other ways.

SUN HAT (LIKED) – ExOfficio BugsAway. I am not a big hat person, but I needed sun protection and this hat did a great job. It was also pretreated with permethrin and has an attached bug net that can be folded away.

TIGHTS (LIKED) – Nike. I used running tights under my shorts on days that started out below 45° F. They worked great and were lightweight. Like the rest of my cold weather gear, I sent them home at Damascus, Virginia and got them back just before going into the Whites in New Hampshire.

LONG-SLEEVED SHIRT (LOVED) – Patagonia Capilene 3 (zippered). This was a great second layer for those cooler mornings – easy to shed once it was warm enough for a short-sleeved shirt.

BEANIE (MEH) – Zpacks (fleece hat). I could take or leave this. It didn't fit great after a couple of washes, but it was warm enough and priced right. Sent home for the summer.

GLOVES (MEH) – Possumdown. Huge shrink factor after putting in a dryer – of course, they were supposed to be air-dried, but who's going to do that on the trail? They developed a hole even though I didn't wear them much. Sent home for the summer.

SLEEP BOTTOMS (LIKED) – Ice Breaker (thermal bottoms, mid-weight merino wool). I sleep warm and only slept in these a handful of times, but they did the job. Sent home for the summer.

SLEEP SHIRT (LOVED) – Smartwool (long-sleeved, mid-weight merino wool). I used this mainly in camp after hiking. Sent home for the summer.

PUFFY JACKET (LOVED) – Mountain Hardwear Ghost Whisperer (hooded, down- filled). The jacket folds into its own pocket and is light and warm enough for all the weather conditions we experienced (when layered).

I kept this jacket, even in the summer, just in case we had a cold night. We didn't.

HIKING SHOES (LOVED – FAVORITE PIECE OF GEAR!) – La Sportiva Wildcats. We were living in Costa Rica when we decided to hike the trail. I had been hiking in Merrell Moabs and liked them fine. The problem was, if they got wet, they stayed wet, so I started to research. When we went back to the US for a trip, we went to REI to try on some shoes. As soon as I slipped on the Wildcats, it was like a fairytale. They fit just right. I bought a pair a half size larger than I typically wear and took them back to Costa Rica. I proceeded to put 500 miles on the shoes and I fell in love.

Once I find something I like, I stick with it, until inevitably the company changes something on the product. La Sportiva are now my daily-wear shoes. I only went through three pairs on the trail and that should be a testament to their durability.

HIKING SOCKS (LOVED) – Darn Tough (merino wool socks – the best socks ever!). I carried three pair of Darn Toughs on our trek – two pairs to hike in and one to sleep in. While the socks do wear out (they got holes in them over 2,200 miles), I was able to get replacements along the way from outfitters that carried them. They have a lifetime, no-fuss warranty.

CAMP SHOES (ALMOST HATE) – Xero Z-Trails. These were followed by a $3 pair of dollar-store flip-flops when the Z-Trails failed. I held such hope for the Xeros, but alas, due to a "manufacturing defect," one of the straps broke on my way down to a water source one night. I had barely put a couple miles on the shoe. It was tough dealing with the company and we went back and forth (they wanted pictures, *etc.*) and finally they sent a replacement.

The $3 flip-flops held up great the rest of the trip.

Another annoying thing about the sandals is that no matter how tight you strap them down, when they are wet, they move around on your feet, especially up or down hills – which would be the entire Appalachian Trail.

RAIN JACKET (LIKED) – Mountain Hardwear Ampato. How to handle rain on a thru-hike is the riddle of all ages. Maybe the answer is unknowable. Being wet is miserable and getting hypothermia is dangerous, so we try. The problem is that rain gear may keep you dry from rain, but you still will get wet with sweat. This Mountain Hardwear jacket is no longer made. It was overkill and a heavy option for the AT, but it was what I already had and I didn't want to buy another one. I used it at the start and got it back at the end.

CHEAPO PONCHO (MEH) – Walmart. I used a cheap poncho for the summer months. I only wore it maybe twice; the rest of the time I just got wet. It billowed with wind in all the wrong places and was uncomfortable to wear.

RAIN KILT (LIKED) – ULA. A rain skirt is a good choice over shorts or pants. Mine went down below my knees, kept me dry and allowed for airflow. Since I almost always wore just shorts, I didn't care much if my lower legs got wet. It also made a great ground cover to sit on when we stopped for a break.

CLOTHES DRY BAG (LIKED) – Zpacks (medium-plus pillow dry bag). It did the job and held all my clean clothes (sleepwear and town-wear). I didn't need the lightness (nor the expense) of cuben fiber. I also didn't need the felt on one side for use as a pillow as I never used it as a pillow. Clothes-sack pillows are hard and uncomfortable.

OTHER

TREKKING POLES (LOVED) – LEKI Corklite. Before our thru-hike, I had never hiked with trekking poles. But during our research, I read story after story of how they can save your butt, literally. For me, they are no longer optional on the AT. They saved me from falling so many times. And the times I did fall, the results would have been worse if the poles hadn't broken some of the fall. The poles are durable and LEKI stands behind their product forever. They are very helpful with warranty claims while on the trail and most issues can be fixed at any outfitter that carries the brand.

For an item I used every single day for six months – and when I say used, I mean abused – they just plain worked. The speedlock system is the best out there. I will (most likely) never need another trekking pole, ever.

CELL PHONE HOLDER (LIKED) – Zpacks (phone zip pouch). The phone carrier barely fit the iPhone 7 Plus, but it was sufficient and it kept my phone on my chest within easy reach.

WALLET (LOVED) – Zpacks (wallet zip pouch). See a Zpacks trend here? They get so much press and their stuff is well made. Looking back, I could have saved so much-money by buying stuff sacks made of silnylon rather than Dyneema. But the wallet I loved and still use. It is small and waterproof, and you can attach a carabiner and clip it anywhere.

CARABINERS (LIKED) – Zpacks (mini carabiners). They are OK. The ones on the outside of our packs started to rust by the end of the trip. They are strong enough for attaching things to your pack, but not for using on your bear bag.

TOILETRIES (MEH) – Dr. Bronner's soap ended up in a hiker box before we left Georgia because it was too much trouble. Hostels have soap for bathing and hand sanitizer was good enough for meal times. Small tube of toothpaste. Toothbrush (three iterations): I used a ridiculous travel toothbrush and then an equally ridiculous cut-down, normal toothbrush before finally coming to my senses and carrying a full-sized toothbrush. Trust me on the small toothbrush thing.

II. Darwin's Gear List

We followed Darwin on YouTube when we were living in Costa Rica and had only just started thinking about doing the AT. His videos provided a wealth of information. He has one for almost any question or subject you may have (seriously). He and his wife, Snuggles, were a huge support for us on our AT thru-hike, and we now consider them friends.

Trail Name: DARWIN

Age: 31

Base weight: 16 pounds (base weight does not include food or water).

Terms: Hiked the AT with his wife, Snuggles, started in 2015 and finished in 2016.

Contact/Follow:

>Youtube.com/darwinonthetrail
>Instagram.com/darwin_onthetrail
>https://darwinonthetrail.com

PACK
Osprey Atmos 65

SHELTER/SLEEP SYSTEM

Big Agnes Copper Spur UL2
EE Revelation 20 quilt
Therm-a-Rest NeoAir Xlite
Sea to Summit Aeros UL pillow

FOOD/WATER SYSTEM
Cook system
Sea to Summit spork
Snow peak Trek 700 titanium mug
SnowPeak LiteMax stove
Zpacks Blast food bag
Sawyer Squeeze water filter
2 Glaceau Smartwater bottles
Platypus GravityWorks 2.0 L dirty reservoir

ELECTRONICS
Black Diamond Spot Headlamp
GoPro HERO5 Session
Poweradd Slim2 charger
StickPic
iPod Shuffle

CLOTHING
Outdoor Research Helium II rain jacket
Mt. Hardwear Ghost Whisperer down jacket

Outdoor Research Transcendent Down Beanie
Nike Pro Combat T-shirt

Nike Pro Combat thermal tights
Darn Tough socks
Buff
Merrell Moab Ventilators
Dirty Girl gaiters

OTHER
Komperdell trekking poles
Therm-a-Rest Z Seat (ass pad)
Zpacks Cuben Stuff Sacks

III. Mystic's Gear List

Chica first cyber met Mystic on Facebook in the Appalachian Trail: Women's Group when she bought "hike" jewelry from Chica's Arm Candy page, and then in person early on in our 2017 AT thru-hike. Mystic will give you a gear list perspective from a woman hiking solo. She used a hammock for her shelter instead of a tent and saved money and weight by dehydrating her meals ahead of time and having her husband mail them to her. Her food for five days only weighed six pounds.

Trail Name: MYSTIC

Real Name: Kim DeGrazia

Age: 56

Base weight: 20.64 pounds (base weight does not include food or water)

Terms: Hiked the AT solo in 2017.

Contact her (she welcomes any questions!):

Email: degraziakim@gmail.com
Private Message on Facebook under "Kim Emon DeGrazia"

PACK
Backpack REI Flash 60
Pack cover Gregory 60

SHELTER/SLEEP SYSTEM
Hennessy Hammock
Tyvek ground cover
EE Revelation 0° quilt
Hennessy 4-season underquilt

FOOD/WATER SYSTEM
MSR Pocket Rocket
Cookpot (1-1/2 liter GSI boiler pot)
Titanium spoon
Platypus 4-liter gravity water filter

ELECTRONICS
Cell phone
Anker 20000 battery pack

CLOTHING
Short-sleeve T-shirt (32° from Costco)
REI convertible pants
Kirkland Signature long-sleeved hoodie
REI wool base layer, top and bottom
Patagonia puffy jacket
Rain gear: Frogg Toggs, men's medium pants & jacket
Underpants (2 pairs)
Socks (one REI, one Smartwool)

Gloves and glove liners (only used once)

OTHER

Toiletries (blister pack, Band-Aids, small sunscreen, small bug spray, ibuprofen, small deodorant, small toothpaste, toothbrush, comb)
Maps: Awol's *AT Guide*, 1/4 at a time.

ACKNOWLEDGEMENTS

Jennifer Evans is a friend and a talented editor. Thank you Jeni – for throwing yourself into this project and using your knowledge and insight to polish it to a high shine.

Thanks to Lynette Hunt for reading through while brandishing her red pen. Lynette – your input made the book better.

Tom Willard and Jennifer Parkinson Cenker were our beta readers. Both have spent considerable time on the Appalachian Trail and we are thankful for their input.

Thanks also goes to Darwin and Mystic, two friends who shared the gear they used on their Appalachian Trail trek.

ABOUT THE AUTHORS

Greg and Jen's philosophy: *work to live; don't live to work.*
Their lifestyle: *chase adventure, not the dollar.*

In 2013, Greg and Jen left the corporate world, where *work more, spend more* was the mantra, and moved to Costa Rica. They became experts on the country and each wrote Amazon best-selling books on the subject of chucking it all and moving to Costa Rica. Jen also has a successful jewelry business, which she started in Costa Rica.

After four years of enjoying Costa Rica and a new fondness for hiking in the mountains of the Central Valley where they lived, the couple was ready for something new. What could be more challenging than spending six months thru-hiking the Appalachian Trail? Starting on Springer Mountain, Georgia and ending on Mount Katahdin, Maine, their thru-hike was the adventure of a lifetime. Along the way they posted daily vlogs about their journey on YouTube.

What's next? Stay tuned as Greg and Jen take on the Camino de Santiago, a 500-mile pilgrimage walk in Spain, in the fall of 2018.

YouTube.com/AppalachianTrailTales
AppalachianTrailTales.com
Facebook.com/AppalachianTrailTales
Instagram.com/AppalachianTrailTales
CostaRicaChicaArmCandy.com

Made in the USA
Columbia, SC
03 November 2018